THE
EVERYTHING
Online Poker Book

Dear Reader,

Years ago, when I was first contemplating playing poker, there was no such thing as online poker. Since I couldn't gain any knowledge or experience online, my father presented me with a stack of extremely outdated poker books. He then advised that I read every one of them before I even thought about stepping one foot into a casino poker room.

I took his sage advice and found myself better prepared and more comfortable than I could have imagined when I sat in on my first poker game. It was Seven-Card Stud on a Thanksgiving night in Las Vegas, and I had a major-league beginner's luck experience. To this day I continue to read poker books.

Many of the books about online poker provide only specific information that appears to be more geared toward a reader who already possesses a basic knowledge and grasp of the game. So it is my intention to provide you with a little knowledge and history of both traditional and online poker, as well as solid advice on dealing with the many situations not usually addressed in poker books. Through reading this book you will learn more than you know now, and you will be a lot more online-poker savvy when you are through.

Here's to many happy, successful, and profitable poker sessions! Remember, no one wins all the time, but when you play correctly, the odds should swing more favorably in your direction!

To my pop, who would have gotten such a kick out of this book, and to my mom, who does. To my brothers, who have never played an on- or offline poker game in their lives. Finally, to Cathy Scott, who taught me everything I know about writing a book and who gave me encouragement and support every step of the way.

• • •

Publisher: Gary M. Krebs

Managing Editor: Laura M. Daly

Associate Copy Chief: Sheila Zwiebel

Acquisitions Editor: Lisa Laing

Development Editor: Katie McDonough

Associate Production Editor: Casey Ebert

Director of Manufacturing: Susan Beale

Associate Director of Production: Michelle Roy Kelly

Prepress: Erick DaCosta, Matt LeBlanc

Layout and Graphics: Heather Barrett, Brewster Brownville, Colleen Cunningham, Jennifer Oliveira

An Everything® Series Book.
Everything® and everything.com® are registered trademarks of F+W Publications, Inc.

Published by Adams Media, an F+W Publications Company
57 Littlefield Street, Avon, MA 02322 U.S.A.
www.adamsmedia.com

ISBN-10: 1-59869-234-8
ISBN-13: 978-1-59869-234-1

Printed in the United States of America.

J I H G F E D C B A

Library of Congress Cataloging-in-Publication Data
is available from the publisher.

PokerRoom illustrations ©PokerRoom.com
Bodog illustrations used with permission from Bodog Entertainment Group S.A.

This publication is designed to provide accurate and authoritative information with regard to the subject matter covered. It is sold with the understanding that the publisher is not engaged in rendering legal, accounting, or other professional advice. If legal advice or other expert assistance is required, the services of a competent professional person should be sought.
—From a *Declaration of Principles* jointly adopted by a Committee of the American Bar Association and a Committee of Publishers and Associations

Many of the designations used by manufacturers and sellers to distinguish their products are claimed as trademarks. Where those designations appear in this book and Adams Media was aware of a trademark claim, the designations have been printed with initial capital letters.

This book is available at quantity discounts for bulk purchases.
For information, please call 1-800-289-0963.

Visit the entire Everything® series at *www.everything.com*

THE
EVERYTHING
ONLINE
POKER BOOK

An insider's guide to playing—
and winning—the hottest
games on the Internet

Helene M. Silverstein

Adams Media
Avon, Massachusetts

Contents

Acknowledgments

I would like to thank June Clark for remembering me when this project came to her attention; my editors, Lisa Laing and Katie McDonough; my dear friends, Joe Morrow and my fuzzy cuzzy Heidi, for letting me bend their ears whenever I became frustrated; and Oscar and Emmie, who sat by my side and kept me sane, showering me with unconditional love and affection.

Top Ten Online Poker Truths and Tips

1. It takes time and patience to master the game of poker.

2. You should always be alert and mentally focused when you play poker.

3. You should never let your bankroll, or lack thereof, dictate your actions.

4. When you flop the nuts, it can only get worse.

5. You should always have a reason to bet on the river.

6. Practice really does make you a better poker player.

7. You shouldn't play just the player or just your cards—play them both.

8. When you think you are beat, you usually are.

9. The cards don't trap you, your incorrect decisions do.

10. "Tells" speak volumes, so always be observant and take good notes.

Introduction

The popularity of online poker is exploding, with two million people playing on more than 300 sites every day! Poker can be watched in the comfort of your own home on several cable networks, and it can even be played without ever having to leave the house. But that's not to say that the highs and lows all poker players experience happen any less frequently when playing online versus playing offline.

In fact, playing online involves some added challenges. For example, many offline players fear that if they can't see their opponents face to face, they will be unable to pick up on "tells"—things like physical quirks and mannerisms, ticks, and eye movements. They feel this puts them at a disadvantage. They're right—when you play online poker, many tells are all but invisible. But, as you'll learn in this book, there are a few tricks that can help you overcome this hurdle.

There are also other aspects of online poker that differ from the physical, tangible casino experience. The Internet poker world is a nameless, faceless environment of virtual tables, icons known as avatars, and made-up screen names. Even the dealer, if there is one, is just for show; the site's computer software algorithms randomly shuffle and deal the cards. And when you play in no-limit online poker games, you will find that there are a lot more all-ins than when you play in offline no-limit poker games. That's because it's psychologically easier to click a mouse than it is to physically move all your chips into the pot.

There are a lot of distractions to deal with when playing online, too. In all probability, most of your online opponents will be watching television, reading, playing in more than one online game at a time, talking on the telephone, or doing something else that disrupts their concentration. If you can think of an online distraction, it's probably happened somewhere at some time.

Whether you are playing poker online or offline, you will find that most people think they are good poker players—and some, very good poker players. Because no one is playing face to face, you'll find that your opponents might be cocky as a means of intimidation. As you will learn from this book, though, this is a common tell. You'll learn how to recognize this and how to adjust your play accordingly.

Learning the basics of poker playing isn't difficult, but it will take a lifetime of continuing education to master the game. A good poker player can never be too informed, too knowledgeable, or too prepared when he is gambling with his hard-earned money. "Know thine enemy" is not just an expression—it's a cardinal rule when it comes to playing poker either online or offline. And that is exactly who you will be surrounded by, enemies who are silently—some not so silently—praying that you will lose your money to them.

Whether you're a risk-taker or a more conservative player, this book will provide you with everything you need to devise a winning strategy to cash in on the online action. Now let's get started and learn how to play some online poker!

Chapter 1

The Evolution of Traditional and Online Poker

There are lots of things you should know before you begin playing poker online, especially if you are used to poker rooms inside the various casinos and card rooms throughout the world. Playing well is not just about strategy and skill; you also need to know poker's story. If you have played before, you may already know some of the information in this chapter. If you are new to poker, then this chapter will give you a good foundation to build upon.

The History of Traditional Poker

Although it has not been verified, the game of poker is believed to have first started around 900 a.d., in China, and evolved from a Chinese domino game played by emperors. However, a more common school of thought on the origins of poker tells us that poker actually evolved in seventeenth century Persia and was played as a game called As Nas. Nas involved a deck of twenty-five cards of five different suits and may have been taught to the French settlers in New Orleans by Persian sailors. The game was played much like today's Five-Card Stud poker and had similarly ranked hands such as three of a kind.

French and German ancestors claim they played a game called Poque, or Pochen, which means to knock, as well as a game called Pochspiel. With Pochspiel, players indicate whether they want to pass or open by rapping on the table and saying "Ich Poche!"

Both Poque and Pochspiel, were played with a deck of twenty cards and involved wagering and a lot of bluffing from the four players as to which of their hands was the most valuable. But it was the card game Poque that came to the United States by way of the French settlers in New Orleans. However, there is some dispute as to whether it was the card game As Nas or Poque that first came to the shores of America.

Fact

On a deck of cards, the King of Spades represents David, King of Israel; the King of Clubs represents Alexander the Great, the King of Macedonia; the King of Hearts represents Charlemagne, King of France; and the King of Diamonds represents Caesar Augustus, Emperor of Rome.

The English claim poker came from a game called Brag, originally spelled Bragg, which descended from Brelan. This game used the concept of bluffing, even though other games by this time also claimed to have incorporated the art of bluffing.

In the 1480s the French began using the terms *spades, clubs, hearts,* and *diamonds*—variations on the Latin words for swords, batons/clubs, cups, and coins, which are the suits of Tarot cards and were used in the early Italian and Spanish card decks.

Poker in the 1800s

Gambling had become a common pastime by the mid-1800s, and it was during this time that the English spread the first fifty-two-card deck and introduced the concept of the flush. Draw poker and stud poker games, which were five-card versions, and the concept of a straight were added along the way during the Civil War era. Unfortunately, even though the game of poker became extremely popular, it was also plagued with dangers from the worst elements of society, including swindlers and cheats who unscrupulously manipulated their marks.

Poker also spread during these times because the West was basically composed of speculators, travelers, and men who enjoyed gambling. These times also gave birth to the professional gambler, whose livelihood flourished. However, these men were thought to have contributed absolutely nothing to society and were therefore viewed as cheats, which was a reputation more than well deserved.

Around 1875 the concept of wild cards came into play. About 1900 the community card popped into poker games, and, in 1925, split-pot poker games appeared on the gambling scene.

The Wild, Wild West

Poker did very well in the Old West. In fact, it thrived. It overcame the popular game of the time, which was Faro, a favorite in saloons and on riverboats among both professional and casual gamblers. In Faro, which is also played with a deck of fifty-two cards, the players bet against a banker/dealer, who draws two cards face-down, one of which will win for the players and the other for the dealer.

Essential

Some people believe that the word *poker* was derived from the word *poke*, which was a slang term for pickpockets, while others feel it came from *hocus-pocus*, a term that was widely used by magicians who also used decks of cards in their magic acts.

Since most everyone carried a side arm in those days, it was a natural marriage made in gambler's heaven: aggressive, confident, frontier men—guns, saloons, and poker.

The Turn of the Twentieth Century

With the birth of the 1900s came the beginning of the age of poker-play credibility and legitimacy. Those who were still a bit rough around the edges continued to enjoy their financial gains, but rarely played in places where the more genteel folk would venture to go.

In 1931 Nevada became the only locale in the United States to legalize casino gambling. And back then, gambling halls and saloons were grimy sawdust joints and a far cry from the mega resort casinos throughout the Nevada of today.

 Fact

Believe it or not, it was once a felony to run a bet in Nevada. Back in 1910 the state of Nevada had made running a betting game a felony but reconsidered their position in 1931.

Nevada remained the only legalized gambling state until 1978 when Atlantic City, New Jersey, jumped on the legalized gambling bandwagon.

Present-Day Poker

Today poker tournaments take place every day all around the world, with anxious gamblers of all legal ages waiting for hours just to get a seat in some of the more popular casino poker rooms and card room games. And all of these establishments are regulated by gambling laws, a far cry from the days of the lawless saloons, riverboats, and back alleys.

Poker is big business and a part of our daily language worldwide. We have all used or heard expressions whose origins are in poker, such as "an ace up your sleeve," "an ace in the hole," "beats me," "calling your bluff," and "when the chips are down."

There is no getting around the fact that poker is here to stay, and it's as close as the click of your mouse!

The Advent of Online Poker

The roots of online poker began in 1994 in Antigua, Bermuda, when the government passed the Free Trade and Processing Zone Act, which opened the door for online gambling under licenses granted by the legislation. To this day, Antigua remains the most popular licensing jurisdiction for online poker site registrations.

InterCasino claims to have been the first online casino to collect real money wagers over the Internet in 1996. However, Planet Poker also claims to have been the pioneer online poker room to go live in 1998, followed by Paradise Poker. By 1999 an estimated 700 online casinos were registered.

Interestingly enough, even though online poker has exploded, the original rake structure of 5 percent to a maximum of $5, put in place by Planet Poker and adopted by most of the other online poker sites, has seen little increase, which is a good thing. (The rake is the percentage that is extracted from the pot to pay for the site's expenses.)

In 1999 Paradise Poker came along and soon became the industry giant. Then, in 2001, Poker Stars came into existence and became very popular, very fast. And the success of Party Poker is a phenomenon all unto itself.

Essential

The future of poker is unlimited, as noted by the frequent, often daily, televised coverage of national and international tournaments, along with all the celebrity poker features and poker tips that these shows provide for the astute poker student.

In 2003, Chris Moneymaker won a seat in the World Series of Poker tournament (WSOP) by playing in, and winning, a $40 online buy-in satellite poker tournament, which guaranteed him a seat in the WSOP. He went on to win the 2003 World Series of Poker tournament, taking home over a million dollars and a WSOP gold and diamond bracelet, and greatly advancing the legitimacy of playing poker online.

In 2004 the increasing popularity of poker due to the "Moneymaker effect" caused the Internet poker-site industry to boom. And as long as there is a game to play, and money to be made, online poker could quite possibly live on forever.

Online Poker Popularity

The popularity of online poker is nothing short of a worldwide phenomenon. Annual revenues generated from online poker action can be estimated at approximately $200 million per month!

You would think that the popularity of poker would eventually level off, but at the rate it is going, that appears to be many years away. And now, with sites such as Empire Poker, Party Poker, and Pacific Poker all looking to become publicly traded, someday soon maybe even you can become a shareholder in your favorite online Internet poker site. Whenever there's a strong potential for making big money, most people just can't resist the lure, and when it comes to online and offline poker, the sky's the limit.

 **Question**

What online poker site had the greatest effect on online poker?
In 1998 Planet Poker was the first online poker site to allow many amateur poker players the opportunity to make a decent living playing poker online, with opponents from all over the world and in the comfort of their own home.

So why is online poker so popular? Think about it. There aren't many other opportunities to make money in the privacy of your own home, a place where you can cuss like a sailor, smoke cigars, and play in your underwear.

Because online poker is a good way to test your skills against actual opponents, and because it gives you the option to use play money when you are practicing or getting the feel for a new or higher limit game, you should have an advantage when considering playing in your first professional card room or casino poker room.

As long as poker remains as popular as it is—and considering all the people in their late teens just champing at the bit to turn twenty-one so that they can play in online and offline poker games—the need for, and success of, the online poker industry will be endless.

Traditional Play Versus Playing Online

It's only natural that playing poker on the computer would be a very different experience from playing it at a casino with living, breathing opponents. If you're used to playing the traditional way, then you may be in for a surprise when you start playing online. You need to learn a whole new repertoire of tricks and strategies to survive in the virtual poker world.

E ssential

In Texas Hold'em and Omaha poker games, there are always community cards dealt to the center of the table and used by all the players in the hand, along with the cards they have been dealt.

For example, when playing traditional poker you rely heavily on "tells" to determine what other players are thinking and plotting. Tells are the little sounds, gestures, or mannerisms a player makes that can give away the value of their hand. Devoted offline card players will tell you that when playing online you will be unable to read your opponent since you can't pick up on their physical tells. It's true that online games prevent you from forming opinions about your opponents' cards due to a lack of body language. However, while many view this lack of physical tells as a disadvantage, there are hundreds of online players who have learned that there are some very telling "tells" to be found when playing poker online.

When you play online all you see of your opponents are their avatars—the cartoonish human icons in place of seated players around a table—and their cards—face up or down, depending on the game you are playing. However, the astute, open-minded offline player will find that there are a few unique characteristics to online play, and that these can be mastered with only a minor tweaking of their player observation skills.

Seat Changes

In casino poker rooms and card rooms, the seat a player chooses may have more to do with his eyesight than anything else. That's because the first seat and the ten seat, along with the five, six, and seven seats, are closer to the middle of the "board" where the community cards are dealt. It is also easier to look forward or left and right than all the way across the table to see player cards. Your seat choice can also reflect your comfort zone, or your superstitions. Just be aware that constant seat changing is usually frowned upon by most poker players.

When a player's favorite seat is not available in an offline game, the player will usually take any available seat and then ask the dealer for a seat change. When it's the actual poker game that the player is unhappy with, however, he will usually request a table change.

When you play poker online you may find that a particular player always plays in one particular seat, and that he will jump around from game to game until he finally finds his favorite seat open. This is a tell to be watchful for. You will probably find that if you lose any money to this player when he is not in his favorite seat, it will not be easy to get your money back if his favorite seat doesn't become available quickly. He might leave the table and look for another where his seat is open.

E Alert

Poker players are a very superstitious lot of people. Lucky seats, lucky charms, and certain hand combinations are just a few of the quirks that you should be looking for. When you see these types of behaviors and characteristics, remember them! They may be of use to you later.

It is very common to see online players moving in and out of seats and games much more frequently than they do when playing in offline poker games. The disadvantage to all this flitting around online is that you don't get to know your competition when they don't hang around long enough.

Table Image

A player's table image is the persona she puts forward when playing. You will spot many different table images when playing online or offline poker. When playing offline you can develop the table image of being a talker, or very quiet, or a solid player, a loose player, a caller, a whiner, a drunk, and so on.

For example, if a player raises every hand no matter what she was dealt, she will be giving off a bully table image. Sometimes players will also use their screen names to intimidate their opponents. If this is the type of table image you want, then make sure a word like "killer" appears in your screen name.

The Speed of Play

The speed of play in a traditional poker game differs greatly from that in an online game. Online poker play is much faster, both in action and in getting seated, than it is when playing in offline games. First, the cards are automatically shuffled in the blink of an eye, and dealt just as quickly. Your chips are moved for you after you click your action on your mouse, and there are never any disputes that need to be addressed.

When playing offline, on the other hand, there is always someone in the game who will dispute the chip count, or feel one of their opponents did not put enough chips in the pot, and so on. These nitpicking complaints slow down the game, causing some players to leave. If you want to contest a hand when playing online, all you have to do is contact the site's member support services, which does not affect the speed of the game.

Always act in a timely fashion when the action comes around to you if you want to avoid annoying your online opponents. Slowing down the game is a tell that shows your opponents that you are distracted, so stay alert and act promptly when it's your turn to act.

Social Pressures

Offline poker action is a more stimulating and social game of cards. Offline poker action allows you to look your opponents right in the eye and speak to them to draw out any of their tells, making it much easier to observe any of their reactions to the pressure. When playing online, however, you may feel compelled to mimic the last action when you see negative things written about you on the chat screen, especially when someone has called an all-in bet.

If you want to keep your opponents off guard, then keep them guessing about your table image. Mix it up, be a little loose when you flop a flush or straight draw, and once in a while, slow play the best hand when you normally would have raised it, to develop the table image of being very difficult to read.

Distractions

Both offline and online poker games come with their share of distractions. In online poker, the biggest distraction might come from the fact that you can play in more than one game simultaneously. When playing in offline games, there are no casino poker rooms or card rooms that would allow you to play in more than one game at a time.

When you play in an offline poker game, the biggest distractions you can expect to experience are the occasional screams when someone's hit the Bad Beat Jackpot, if the poker room offers one. The Bad Beat Jackpot usually consists of all player money that the dealer has dropped into the bad beat chip slot on the poker table. This amount is usually fifty cents to a dollar per hand played.

Most offline poker rooms require a minimum hand of Aces full of Jacks to be beaten by four Jacks, or better, in order for the hands to qualify as the bad beat. If you have four Jacks and your opponent has four Kings, you are the bad beat and would win a larger portion of the bad beat jackpot. The winner of the hand, the four Kings, would get a smaller portion, and the pot. In some poker rooms, the dealt-in players at the table where the bad beat was would also get a percentage of the jackpot, while in other poker rooms the bad beat jackpot is paid out to everyone who was playing in the same game when the bad beat was hit.

Many of your online opponents will likely be doing other things while playing poker, such as talking on the phone or watching television. This is a great thing for you, as a distracted player is an easy player to take advantage of. Use this knowledge and play your hands accordingly to build—and win—the biggest possible pots.

Other distractions could include the antics of an on-tilt player whose winning hand just got beat on the river.

Fact

Studying your opponents' betting habits is an excellent way to help you decide your play when the action gets around to you and you find yourself faced with a decision that can have a major effect on your bankroll.

Abusive Players

The worst that can happen to an abusive offline player is having his chips picked up from the table, being cashed out, and being asked to leave the poker room. However, if he is excessively verbally or physically abusive he may find himself banned from a poker room. You want the table image of a solid poker player, not a loudmouthed loser who's been banned from some online and offline poker rooms.

When you play online and find that your temperature is beginning to rise, you can vent your frustrations by simply screaming whatever profanities come to mind in the privacy of your own home without fear of being ejected from the game. Try this in a casino poker room or card room and you will find that your days there are numbered.

⚡ Alert

Don't be surprised to see yourself instantly voted off a table the minute you click into a game. Many online jerks enjoy doing this, and they only want to get a rise out of you. Just ignore them and play in a timely manner, so no one will be able to pick up on your tells.

Differences in Online and Offline Etiquette

There is no doubt about it, you can get away with more antics in the privacy of your own home than you can in a casino poker room or professional card room. Poor etiquette is by far the second biggest bone of contention for many online poker players—the first being not acting in a timely manner. It's important that you know what's accepted and what's not before you step into an online poker game.

Chatting Guidelines

Just as you can talk to the people at your table when you play poker in a card room, you can also "chat" with your opponents in an online game. To chat with your poker tablemates all you have to do is type on the bar in the chat box and then hit Return. Instantly you will see your words in the dialog box, as will everyone else. Your chat box will also give running commentary describing all action, along with table chat. It will tell you what cards you were dealt, what the flop is, and every player's action.

When players want to vote someone off the table, you will see the player's screen name and how many votes have been cast against them in the chat box. To mute or vote off a player, simply click on their avatar and a window will open offering you the option of muting their chat or voting them out of the game.

Question

Can I chat about a hand that is currently in progress if I'm no longer in the hand?
No. You should never chat about any hand in progress for two reasons. First, chatting about a hand in progress is inappropriate, and second, it can be construed as a form of cheating by players still in the hand.

One thing you definitely want to avoid if you don't want to be voted out is giving unsolicited poker advice to your opponents. Players want to see your action—they don't want to hear your thoughts. Keep them to yourself.

Mind Your Manners

Are you the type of person who curses on a regular basis? Do you like making jokes and using sarcasm? If so, you might want to curb these habits when you enter an online poker game. Many people find cursing disrespectful, and sarcasm and jokes don't always go over correctly when typed on a screen. Try visualizing someone you respect behind one of those avatars and then conduct your chat dialogue accordingly.

Any words or vulgar expressions that other players might find offensive can get you voted out of a game. This can include things like off-color jokes or stories and name-calling. What's worse, too much inappropriate chatting can get you booted out of the game and off the site by the poker site's member support services team.

When you first arrive at a game you may notice that the chat is being directed toward you. Don't ignore your opponents; give a casual greeting like "hi" or "howdy." If you prefer being a nonverbal player, simply remain silent, or keep your responses short, and your lack of chat will usually be respected.

Generally speaking, you should try to be minimally social when you enter or leave a poker game—online or off. It's the right thing to do, and very good for your table image.

Stepping Away from a Game

Whenever you need to step away from the game, just click "Sitting Out" rather than inconsiderately wasting the players' time while the computer's software keeps beeping at you to act. In both online and offline games you are usually given at least forty minutes to return to the table before you are taken out of the game. If you're leaving a game for good and not just for a bathroom break, it's polite to let your tablemates know. Say "later," "bye," or whatever you feel comfortable with. This way, your opponents won't be waiting in vain for you to return.

E Fact

It's a given: Nature will always call, whether you are playing in an online poker game or in a casino card room. The best time to leave the game for a few minutes is when the blinds are getting closer and the advantage of your seat position has diminished greatly.

If you find yourself picked up when playing in a casino poker room or professional card room, you will be placed at the top of the waiting list when you return to the poker room. Online players simply have to click back into the game or go to another one.

The Online Poker Community

All different kinds of people from all different places and backgrounds play online poker. Though you probably won't realize it, you may end up playing with your family members, clergy, friends, doctors, and lawyers. You might also find yourself at a virtual table with some very experienced or even famous poker players. It's a good idea to become familiar with these people's screen names, as they're the ones who will take your money the quickest.

Following is a list of screen names used by some of the world's greatest poker champions. Just knowing the player behind the screen name will automatically give you a leg up on your opponents. However, keep in mind that, like any other online poker player, the poker pros may also have more than one name, so it is up to you to recognize and keep track of them when you play online. And because many of these players use their real names, and because being able to get the name you request may be more difficult than you think, due to supply and demand, many poker players will not change their screen names. However, they may use a different screen name from one online Internet site to another.

Here are just a few examples of the poker professionals who use screen names other than, or in conjunction with, their real names:

- David Benyamine: magicpitch
- Doyle Brunson: TexDolly
- T. J. Cloutier: J9ofClubs
- Hoyt Corkins: EasyH
- Phil Gordon: Tallphil
- Gus Hansen: broksi
- Phil Ivey: joe buttons
- Howard Lederer: the shrike
- Mike Matusow: MrPokeJoke and dill pickle

The following poker pros are commonly seen online using their real names. However, be assured that they also have well-concealed screen names that they use when playing in high-stakes online poker games:

- Todd Brunson: Todd Brunson
- Mike Caro: Mike Caro
- Annie Duke: Annie Duke
- Layne Flack: Layne Flack

- Phil Hellmuth: Phil Hellmuth
- Kathy Leibert: Kathy Leibert
- Tom McEvoy: Tom McEvoy

These are just the tip of the iceberg—many well-known poker players play in online poker games. It is up to you to be aware of them by maintaining a list that you can consult whenever you learn a new online pro's screen name or think one has just popped into your game.

Chapter 2

Getting Started

Now that you've had an introduction to poker history and the differences between traditional and online poker, it's time to start getting yourself ready to play online! Before you hop into an open seat at a table, though, you need to follow a few preliminary steps. First, of course, is choosing a site to play on. Most online poker sites will require you to sign up and create an account, as well as set up a system for betting. This chapter covers all the basics to get you started playing online poker.

Selecting an Online Poker Site

Finding the right online poker site means visiting a lot of different sites to check out what features each site has to offer. For example, you should be looking for a variety of games and good action (lots of betting), as well as checking to see if they offer both play-money and real-money games.

Tips for Choosing a Site

Choosing a site might not seem like a big decision, but you will be registering and creating an account with each site you choose, so there is a level of commitment involved. Before you click the button to download a site's software, consider the following points:

- **Play money is good practice.** If you are new to online poker it's important that you start out by playing on sites that offer play-money games and tournaments. These games will offer you the opportunity to learn the basics while getting accustomed to the site.

- **It's a personal choice.** While some sites are better than others, there really isn't a site that's "the best." Like choosing a favorite restaurant, picking a poker site depends on your individual taste.
- **Comfort is key.** Make sure you are comfortable with the graphics and avatars seated around the poker table. Remember, you will be looking at your computer screen for several hours at a time.
- **The site should meet your qualifications.** Make sure the site offers all the games and dollar limits you want to play, along with tournaments that interest you. Also check to see if the tournament structure offers single-table tournaments, two-table tournaments, multi-table tournaments, freeroll tournaments, and satellites into the World Series of Poker tournament.
- **Betting limits are important.** If you're going to be betting on games, make sure you have options, such as fixed-limit, pot-limit, and no-limit games.
- **Sites should be secure.** Make sure the site you choose is secure, especially if you plan to gamble with your savings account.

Most importantly, make sure you play on sites that are comfortable and where you tend to do well. If you find yourself running cold, that could be a good time to start seeking out a new online poker site. Never be afraid to make a site change—you'll be glad you did it later.

Question

I like the site I'm playing on, but it doesn't offer a game I just learned to play. What should I do?
You can contact your member support services team and request that they spread the game. If this is not an option, just surf the Internet and find another site that fits all your poker needs, and play there.

Poker Sites for Mac and Linux Users

For several years Mac and Linux users were out of luck when it came to downloading poker sites to their computers. That is, until a number of online poker rooms started offering a no-download Java client that is compatible with both Macs and Linux. However, today many sites offer complete versions of their software for Mac and Linux users.

Following are some sites that have offered Mac and Linux options all along:

- Full Tilt Poker (*www.fulltiltpoker.com*)
- GamesGrid Poker (*www.gamesgrid.com*)
- HoldemPoker.com (*www.holdempoker.com*)
- Pacific Poker (*www.pacificpoker.com*)
- PokerRoom.com (*www.pokerroom.com*)

Setting Up an Account

Getting started is as easy as typing the site you are interested in into your browser. If you haven't decided which poker site you'd like to use, check out Appendix D in the back of the book. This appendix offers a list of popular online poker sites, complete with a description of each. Once you've chosen a site, just type it into your browser and click Go. When the site's home page appears on your computer screen, simply click on the "Download Now" hyperlink, and the site's software will download to your computer. Software downloads on Internet poker sites should always be free. If the site you've chosen charges for software downloads, keep looking until you find one that doesn't.

Once you've downloaded the software you will see a clearly visible link that could say "Register," "New Players Sign Up Here," "Get Started," or "Sign Up." Clicking this link should allow you to sign up for access to the site.

Now you are ready to fill in the required fields on the registration form. In most cases you will need to fill in your name, complete mailing address, e-mail address, and date of birth. You will also be asked if you are of legal age to gamble. Finally, you'll be asked to select a

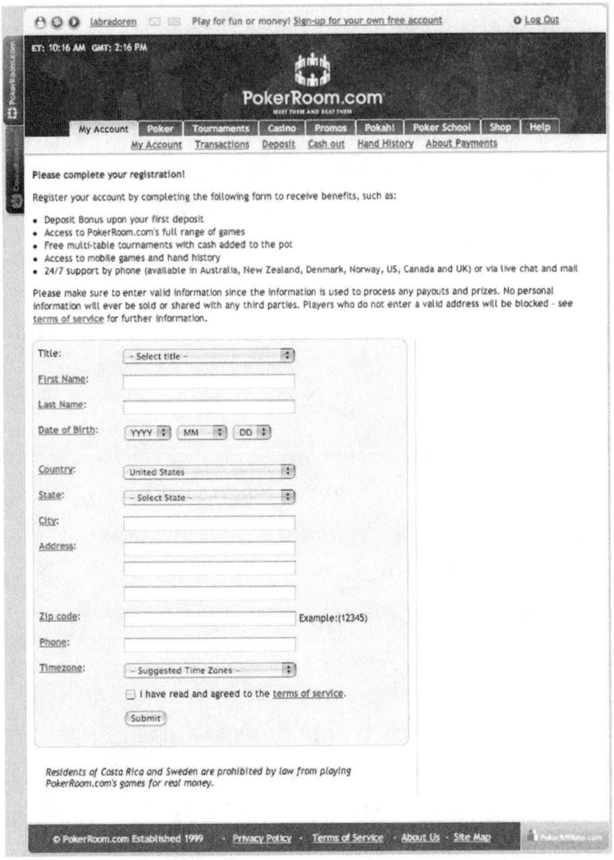

Figure 2.1 PokerRoom.com sign-up page

screen name, nickname, or handle that you want to use, as well as a password.

Choosing a screen name sounds simple, but it is not something to be taken lightly. For one thing, you don't want your screen name to act as a tell for your opponents. It's best to project a positive image with your screen name—or at least a neutral one. Also, be sure you have backup names ready in case the screen name you have your heart set on is already in use.

Stay away from names that indicate gender, such as prettylady or toughguy. Names like these will give your tablemates preconceived notions about you that might make it easier for them to guess what

Figure 2.2 How screen names appear on screen (Bodog.com)

moves you'll make in the game. Something more neutral, like new-yorker, is better.

Also avoid names that imply that you are manic or deranged unless that's your misguided intention. Your screen name is just as major a tell as when a player only raises with pocket Aces. If you choose a non-gender-specific name, you can keep your opponents guessing, rather than giving them knowledge they can use against you.

 Alert

When you enter a poker game, the other players might greet you with rapid-fire text messages. It's their way of detecting as many tells about you as they can. It's important that you offer no information about yourself or your play to your opponents. It's equally important to find out as much about them and their play as you possibly can.

Once you've chosen a screen name and have entered in all your other personal information, you'll be asked to agree to the Terms and Conditions. You must check "Yes" or "I Agree" to play on that site.

Next, decide whether you are going to play with play money or open an online account with real money. These options should be clearly explained on the site, making it easy for you to choose one or the other. (You'll read more about betting later in this chapter.) If you aren't quite ready to play yet and would like to simply observe a couple of games, that's fine too.

Choosing a Game

Once you've set up your account it's time to select a game to play. The best games to start with are those you feel most comfortable playing. If you've never played before, it's a good idea to start with a game that you're at least partially familiar with. For example, if you've watched Texas Hold'em poker tournaments on television, that's probably your best bet as a beginner.

E ssential

Always check your ego at the door before you sit in on any online or offline poker game. Arrogance is a tell that is easily picked up on by opponents. You may think you're the best poker player in cyber-space, but you also might be playing against an actual world poker champion!

Following is a list of some of the games you'll find on online poker sites. These games can usually be found in both limit and no-limit variations, and they will all be discussed in detail later in the book:

- Texas Hold'em
- Omaha
- Omaha High
- Omaha High-Low
- Seven-Card Stud
- Seven-Card Stud High
- Seven-Card Stud High-Low

Additional, less popular games such as Five-Card Draw Poker, Razz Poker, and Crazy Pineapple will be discussed in Chapter 11.

Picking a poker game is universally the same on all sites. After you log onto the site, you're in the lobby and able to see tabulated listings of all the games and tournaments offered. Click on the poker game you prefer to play, study the games listed, and then highlight the game that most interests you.

Your Bankroll

Playing online poker can be fun, even exciting, but many people lose more money than they can afford to when they are comfortably playing on a cyberspace poker site in the privacy of home. This may be, in part, due to the fact that losses in the virtual world never seem as bad as they do in the real world. Or perhaps it's because the losses aren't as physically immediate. The average online poker player does not feel the pain that offline players feel when the chips that were just in his hand are now being stacked in front of an opponent.

Online poker can be a very costly hobby if you don't keep close track of your wins and, especially, your losses. If you find that you are consistently losing more than you are winning, perhaps it's time to take a breather from the game until you feel your skill level and luck have changed.

⚡ Alert

If you can't afford the financial losses, then play poker in the play-money games. Otherwise you will be playing with scared money, which is money that you cannot afford to lose, especially if it's for your rent or mortgage.

Maintaining an adequate bankroll can be difficult when you find yourself running bad. Everyone runs bad once in a while, but it's how you handle yourself during these bad spells that can make or break you. So here's a question you might want to ask yourself when Lady

Luck seems to be elusive: Just how much more money am I willing to invest without risking the quality of my life?

First, you have to figure out exactly how much money you can afford to lose without straining your finances. Then ask yourself what game and limit you feel you do best in. Then decide if you would rather play in tournaments or cash games. One of the benefits of tournament play is that you know exactly how much money it will cost you to enter. And if you are lucky enough to finish in the money, you will be well on your way to feeding your starving online cash account.

If you do not know how to figure out how much money you should have on deposit, one school of thought is that it should be ten times the amount of the big blind. Therefore, if you play in a $4/$8 Limit Texas Hold'em game, you would need at least $80 at your disposal. Another school of thought says that you should have at least 100 times the small blind in your account. Then you would need a deposit of $400 in your account for the same game.

 ## Question

I want to play in a no-limit game but I'm afraid that I could lose all my money in just one hand. Is that possible?
You may very well lose all your money in just one hand, and quite possibly the one and only hand you play. So to protect your bankroll, play only in games where you feel comfortable, play only the premium cards, and gamble only with money you know you can afford to lose.

Tournament play also needs a bankroll, and this bankroll should be larger than your non-tournament poker games if you plan on playing in the better and larger buy-in tournaments on a regular basis.

The size of your online poker account should depend on how much disposable income you are willing to invest, what limit you're playing in, and whether or not you can withstand bad beats with a modicum of self-control. If not, you could be setting yourself up for losses that you cannot afford.

The Benefits of Play Money

Most, if not all, Internet poker sites offer their players two options: You can play with either real money or play money. Just how much play money they give you will vary from site to site. In most cases, if you lose it all, you can usually get one daily reload. You can also get play-money points as a bonus for getting your family and friends to register on the site, and as a part of various promotional offers.

Playing with play money is an excellent way to hone your game skills and to get a feel for the higher limit games and tournament play, and it gives you a breather when you're on tilt from running bad but still want to play. For poker newbies, playing with play money is

Figure 2.3 Signing up for a free account on PokerRoom.com

a smart thing to do. The play-money games enable you to practice without fear of going broke. Just keep in mind that players in the play-money games tend to play more loosely than players in real-money games, so be prepared to see a lot of raising and all-ins.

Essential

You will always play more hands per hour playing in online games than you will playing in offline games. Hand for hand, the speed of online play is about the same for play-money games and real-money games.

Also try using your time wisely when playing in the play-money games by training yourself to be aware of tells and to condition yourself to take good notes. By doing this you will have ingrained good observation skills into your style of play and be ready to move on to real-money games.

Chapter 3

Preparation Before You Play

By this point you should have chosen an online poker site and created an account for yourself. You're almost ready for the fun part: starting to play! This chapter covers all the remaining information you need to get in on an online poker game. First you'll read about choosing a poker table and a good seat, and then you'll get a refresher course on the basic hand rankings in poker, as well as some helpful hints for your first game. Good luck!

Choosing a Table

In the "lobby" of your online poker site you will find menu links to all the games available along with the site's tournament calendar. Pick the game or tournament that you want to play, highlight it to view the screen names of players already in that game, and note their chip count. You will also be able to find the play-money tables listed separately.

After you decide what limit to play, and whether to play with real money or play money, simply click on "Enter the game" or "Go to game" button. *Voila!* Through the magic of the Internet you're in that poker room in real time. Don't click yourself into the game just yet, though. First learn about your future opponents' play by taking a few minutes to study some hands before the players have a chance to study you.

When you cruise the available games in the limit you plan to play, you are able to see exactly who is playing in which games, thus allowing you to avoid any players you would rather not play against.

You should also be able to pick up on people who are playing in multiple games by noting whether the same screen names appear in more than one poker game.

A waiting list sign-up box is located just below the screen that shows the list of players in a particular game. Ideally, you don't want to wait too long. If there are only one or two names on the list ahead of you, you might put your name on that list and then go to the game, with notebook in hand, and study the players. Look to see how many call to see the flop and whether some call to see every flop. You will also be able to see the total number of chips they have in front of them and the size of the pot.

Question

Will I be able to choose a specific character to suit my nickname, or am I stuck with the avatars seated around the virtual poker table?
There are a few sites that do allow you to choose a character image that matches your nickname when you log onto the site. Bodog Poker even allows you to upload a photo to use for your onscreen avatar.

Once you gain more experience playing online poker, you'll be in a better position to choose your games wisely. You will also have a better understanding of some of your future opponents' play as you pick up on their tells. Any knowledge of weak players in an online or offline poker game is a plus. Use this knowledge wisely and take advantage of any player weaknesses whenever the opportunity arises.

Take a Seat

It's important to understand that no single seat around any virtual— or felt-and-leather—poker table is any luckier than any other seat. When you're running hot (winning), you can change seats after each hand and still continue to win. When you're running cold (losing), you can make a seat change into what had been a very hot seat for a previous player, yet that person's rush (winning streak) doesn't continue for you. That's because there are no guarantees in poker. Never underestimate the value and importance of the luck factor.

Essential

Some players choose their seats according to the avatar pictured on their computer screens. There are usually more male than female characters of all ethnicities, shapes, and sizes seated around the table. The best seat at the table is the dealer button, the seat that has just completed both blinds and is last to act before the blind's options. But you only get this seat position once every round of play.

In offline poker games, some players pick specific seats for flop visibility; however, this is never the case when you play online poker. Every seat has the same visibility factor. And since the action moves around the table clockwise, there is no particular advantage to sitting in one seat versus another . . . or is there? This is where your observation skills come into play. When you sit quietly in the background and watch the play around the table before entering the game, hopefully you will notice who plays more aggressively and who plays tight. So the ideal seat position at this table would be any seat after the loose players but before the tight players, so that you will know to either fold the aggressive players' action or raise to knock out the tight player.

But don't be surprised if a seated player is able to seat jump into the same seat you've had your eye on before you get the chance. Just knowing that this player is also watching everyone is a tell.

After you click on the avatar of an open seat, you will see, at the bottom of your screen, a bar showing you how much play money or real money you have in your account. Simply type in how much you want to use as your bankroll and click. The amount will appear under your screen name printed above your avatar at the table. As players win and lose pots, their bankroll totals will change accordingly, which you also see.

Then click on "Sit In" in the boxes to the bottom right on your computer screen. This is usually close to your bankroll bar and where you should also find options such as "Leave," "Lobby," and "Cashier."

 Fact

Your screen name and bankroll total will become highlighted when it's your turn to act. You will also hear ringing or buzzing sounds when it's your turn if you are not moving quickly enough. Take that as a warning; if it happens more than once, maybe it's time to take a break, because your attention span is obviously waning.

In one of the top corners of your computer screen you should find the number of the hand just played and the number of the hand that is in play. At the bottom of your screen, usually in the center, you will see the amount of the current bet, the size of the pot, and the amount of the rake that is taken from the pot. The rake is the percentage that is extracted from the pot by casino poker rooms, card rooms, and online poker sites, and it pays for the offline or online site's expenses. This amount can vary, but it is usually anywhere from $3 to $5 and is taken from the pots in play-money and real-money games.

Also toward the bottom of your computer screen you will find "Fold," "Check," "Bet," "Check/Fold," "Check/Call Any," and "Bet/Raise Any," any of which you simply click with your mouse to initiate your action. Most sites give the option to click your action in advance if you know, for example, that you will call any amount that's bet ahead of you.

The Basic Hand Rankings in Poker

Before you even thinking about playing poker, you should know what cards make what basic poker hands, what beats what, and how they are ranked. Following are the universal poker hands ranked from the highest possible hand (1) to the lowest possible hand (9). Refer back to these descriptions as often as you need to until you've got them memorized.

1. **Royal flush:** A straight from the Ten to the Ace with all five cards being of the same suit. The only example of royal flush would be A-K-Q-J-10, all of the same suit.

2. **Straight flush:** Any five sequential cards, all of the same suit. An example of a straight flush would be Kh-Qh-Jh-10h-9h, also called a King-high heart straight flush. The lowest possible straight flush would be 5-4-3-2-A, all of the same suit, also known as a wheel.

3. **Four of a kind:** Any four cards of the same rank. An example of four of a kind would be Q-Q-Q-Q or 8-8-8-8.

4. **Full house:** Any three cards of the same rank, along with any two cards of the same rank. An example of the best possible full house is A-A-A-K-K, also called Aces full of Kings. The lowest possible full house is 2-2-2-3-3.

5. **Flush:** Any five cards of the same suit but not in consecutive order. The highest card in the five suited cards determines how high the flush is. An example of an Ace-high heart flush would be Ah-9h-6h-5h-2h.

6. **Straight:** Any five sequential cards of different suits. With straights, the Ace can be either high, for the Ace-high straight, or low, for the wheel. Examples of these straights would be A-K-Q-J-10 and 5-4-3-2-A, off-suit.

7. **Three of a kind:** Any three cards of the same rank. An example of three of a kind would be K-K-K or 8-8-8.

8. **Two pair:** Any two cards of the same rank, along with another two cards whose ranks are the same. An example of two pair would be J-J-10-10.

9. **One pair:** Any two cards of the same rank. An example of one pair would be K-K.

If none of these hands appears after the river has been checked or bet, then the highest cards in a player's hand will win. If both players hold an Ace, then the rank of their second card, or the board if it's higher, comes into play. If one player holds an Ace with a King and the other an Ace with a Queen, then the Ace with the King kicker will win the pot. So, if there are no pairs, the player with the highest card in hand wins.

E Fact

A bad beat is a losing hand that usually occurs on the river, when the final card is revealed. And even though, nine times out of ten, this hand should have held up after you made it as expensive a draw as possible for your opponent, when you lose it on the river, it can be devastating to your ego and bankroll.

Advice for Those Who Are New to Poker

This section is geared toward those people who have only been playing poker for the past six months or so. It will give you vital information on detecting tells, explain the value of good note-taking, and provide many additional useful tips.

It's All about the Tells

Offline players watch their opponents' eyes and look at their facial expressions and tics, along with hand movements and how they handle their chips. They take note of who peeks down at their down cards, telegraphing that they can't remember their hand.

Others may appear anxious, or might demonstrate nervous body language such as shaking legs, tapping feet, eye twitches, or dry mouth.

But this is not quite as simple when playing online, because the avatars seated around the virtual poker table do not flinch. So you may have to adjust your definition of the word *tell* in order to play your online poker game more effectively.

⚡ Alert

You are "playing tight" when you only play the premium cards, such as pocket Aces and Kings. But when you play tight online, you are more able to get good action that you might not have gotten when pegged as a tight player in offline poker games.

When you play poker online, be sure that you play with good starting hands and base your actions on your cards and on the cards you see on the board. Then begin to analyze your opponents' actions, such as their betting habits, or lack thereof, which can speak volumes.

Following are some suggestions for detecting tells in your online opponents. You might want to commit them to memory and act accordingly when presented with these types of situations and playing patterns in both online and offline poker games.

- Be aware of all opponents who appear distracted.
- Identify and remember the opponents who delay their action, then check. This could indicate that your opponent has a weak hand. However, when he waits to act and then calls the bet, it can also mean that he has a strong hand. This is why it is very important to know your opponents' betting habits.
- Observe when opponents call too quickly. Doing this may mean that she has a weak hand, though it could also mean that her hand is strong but she wants you to think it's weak in the hope that you will raise.

- Be aware when an opponent bets or raises without missing a beat. This is especially true when he bets quickly on the turn or river, and it is usually a very strong tell that your opponent is holding a very strong hand. However, he is probably hoping that you will think he is trying to steal the pot with a bluff while he prays that you will call or raise him.
- Know that an instant check usually is a sign of weakness. When an online opponent checks, he usually only has a drawing hand, or no hand at all. However, if you are last to act, and everyone ahead of you has checked, then you might want to take advantage of your position and bet.
- When your opponent checks, the flop but calls any bets on the flop, then comes out betting on a turn card that couldn't have possibly helped anyone's hand, this usually means her hand is weak but she wants you to think just the opposite. Or it could mean that she is slow playing a high pair, two pair, or a set. This is why knowing how your opponents play is vital in knowing how to play your own hand.
- Always be aware of the opponent who check-raises you. This can mean weakness when there are several other players still left in the hand. However, if any of your opponents have checked quickly, then you raise just as quickly, but be very cautious of a re-raise.

The Importance of Note-Taking

When it comes to detecting tells from your opponents, the importance of good note-taking cannot be emphasized enough if you want to be successful. It's surprising how many offline players take notes. So if you plan on playing with your hard-earned cash, then note-taking is an essential tool for your financial success. Besides, without good notes and financial records, how will you know if you are winning or losing, especially if you tend to play in multiple games or on more than one site?

Most sites offer a note-taking feature, and you should start using it the very first time you observe or play in any play-money or real-money games. You are also able to download your notes to your hard drive. Just contact your member support services team and ask them how to do this, and they will e-mail you back step-by-step directions.

E ssential

Any player who says that keeping records and notes is the sign of a rank amateur is either deceiving himself or attempting to throw you off your game by making you question your actions. Do not fall for this psychological ploy—maintain excellent note-taking and financial records.

A Few More Online Poker Tips

Now you've refreshed your memory on the basic poker hands and the importance of detecting tells and taking notes. But there are a few more tips that apply specifically to the online poker game. If you've played poker in casinos but never online, the following points will give you final pieces of the puzzle:

- Start out playing in the play-money games.
- When playing with real money, start at the lower limit buy-ins and play in limit games and tournaments.
- Spend time observing the play of potential opponents to get a sense of the game's action and to pick up on any tells.
- Before playing in higher limit real-money games, play in the higher limit play-money games to get the feel of the game and the action.
- Know that you will not be the next World Series of Poker tournament winner overnight. It takes time, patience, and a lot of practice.
- Do not confuse your bankroll with your ability to play. Bad beats can wreak havoc on even the best of poker player's finances.

- Trust in yourself enough to keep your money on account and try not to cash out for at least six months while you continue to work on, and improve, your game.
- Concentrate on the game and turn off all distractions. However, music is acceptable as long as it does not cause you to get up and dance around or fall asleep.
- Steer clear of playing in multi-table games when you are still a beginner. It's hard enough to concentrate on one game effectively without having to pay attention to two or three other games simultaneously.
- Never forget that it's easy to leave a game when you are winning, but very difficult to leave when you are losing.

Remember, no matter how honed your online and/or offline poker skills are, luck is still a major factor in winning any poker game, along with skill and patience. Take your poker experience one hand at a time. Before long you'll be the player your opponents are looking out for.

Chapter 4

Online Poker Cautions

Poker is a fun game, and you'll certainly enjoy your experience playing in card rooms and online. But as with any game that involves betting, there are some warnings that should not be ignored. When you sign up on a poker site you offer up your personal information, including financial information, when you create an account. The last thing you want is to find yourself being cheated or unwittingly breaking any laws. This chapter covers the technical and legal aspects of playing poker online.

The Legal Side of Betting Online

Many people wonder if virtual betting is legal. In truth, this has been a point of contention since online gambling was born. Since (at the time that this book was written) there have been no legal precedents and no American citizen has ever been arrested, let alone brought to trial, convicted, or sentenced for gambling online, most people assume that it is legal. Still, there are those who take the opposite stance. Those who argue that online gambling is illegal take their interpretation from the Federal Wire Wager Act. Parts of the Wire Act can be interpreted as barring online poker; in particular, the section of the Act that makes it a crime for anyone in the business of gambling to use a wire that crosses a state line for the purpose of sending information that could be helpful in placing bets. However, there are not yet any legal precedents on which to base this argument.

In 1961, then–U.S. Attorney Robert Kennedy proposed the Wire Act as part of his War on Crime campaign. Initially it was designed to help the states enforce the prohibition of betting on sports events and races through telephone lines. However, the Wire Act explicitly does not cover the transmission of information assisting in the placing of bets or wagers on a sporting event or contest from a state or foreign country where betting on that event or contest is legal. And so the door opened for Nevada, which, at the time, allowed betting on horse races taking place in other states when they needed a way to receive results of those races for their gamblers in a timely fashion.

Essential

There are laws now in place to ensure that those who own and operate gambling Web sites can be restricted to not only where their business is located, but also where their servers and computers can be located.

So what does the savvy entrepreneur do to create an online poker Web site? He simply bases his online casino outside the jurisdiction of the United States government. And where do many of these people go to set up their businesses? Here are some examples: Bodog Poker is based in Costa Rica, CDPoker is based in Antigua, Hollywood Poker is based in Canada, InterPoker is based in Cyprus, and Pacific Poker is based in Gibraltar. These foreign governments now reap the huge tax revenues that the companies gladly pay to be able to operate their extremely profitable sites.

However, gambling regulations are traditionally decided by the individual states and not the federal government. If you are playing online in a state that is not gambling friendly, such as Utah (which outlaws gambling in all forms), rather than a state where gambling is permitted, the legalities are a bit blurred.

If the legality issue is something that concerns you, you might want to get online and surf the Web for your state's Web site and look for links regarding the gambling laws. But unless every computer has a Big Brother feature installed and programmed to alert the law every time you log onto an online poker site, then states such as New York and Washington, which both want a law that prohibits Internet gambling, will have a difficult time when it comes to pursuing, charging, and prosecuting violators.

Are Online Poker Sites Safe?

Security and privacy are important concerns when you are playing with real money, so you should be sure that the site you are planning to register on has the mechanisms in place that will prevent criminals from exploiting players and the site. Mechanisms like secure servers and the types of random number generators (RNG) they have are important. The better the RNG, the higher the level of unpredictability in the cards being played.

Well-run sites have all the safety measures in place that make it difficult for even their employees to access any information beyond the minimum that they would need to perform their tasks proficiently.

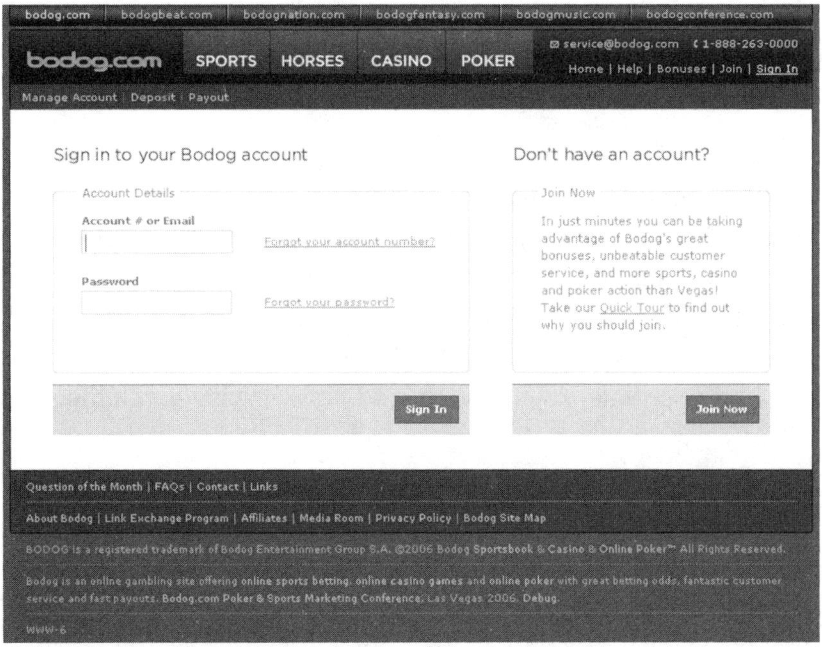

Figure 4.1 Without your account or e-mail address and password, access will be denied.

Information such as legal names, addresses, telephone numbers, bank accounts, credit cards, and NETeller and FirePay accounts are not available to the site's employees. But to be sure of a particular site's safety, read their privacy policy, maybe even print out a copy for your records, before you begin to play on that site.

Although there is very little information available on online poker rooms and the success of their player security programs, there have been no publicly reported breaches of any online poker databases to date. But keep in mind that the smaller sites have fewer resources and are therefore much more likely to become vulnerable to either an electronic or insider attack.

 Question

Can a niche poker room site be safe?
Yes, especially if they have taken all the precautions the larger sites have taken. But remember, niche sites are new and still growing, so be sure to inquire about whether they have all the essential safety measures in place.

It's natural—and smart—to be a bit wary of any Internet transactions. This goes not only for things like betting but also for buying clothes, paying bills, or doing anything else that requires financial and personal disclosures. Stick to the bigger, more well-established Internet poker rooms and you should feel safe and secure—and able to spend your time playing poker and not worrying about the site's security.

Placing a Secure Bet

If it is your intention to open up an online real-money account, then point and click on the hyperlink designated for New Accounts. Usually a screen will appear that asks you questions similar to the ones you are asked when you arrange for automatic payments to be taken from or deposits made to your checking account.

Figure 4.2 Placing a safe online deposit on Bodog.com

A popular way to electronically transfer funds into your online account is through a secure online money transfer service such as NETeller. Almost all Internet poker sites offer NETeller, which has an excellent track record—as does FirePay—for establishing your online poker account. However, it is all a matter of preference, so only you can decide which method of money transfer works best for you.

Keep in mind that funding an online poker account is nothing like playing in a casino poker room or card room, where you merely walk up to the poker room's cashier cage, hand them your money, and then walk to your table with a rack of chips in your hand.

Be aware that setting up your online real-money poker account transaction can take between two to four business days to be completed. However, with NETeller, you are able to immediately transfer money to and from your checking account after you have registered your bank information with them.

⚡ Alert

There has been a lot of talk lately about changing the laws regarding the use of credit cards and savings and checking accounts for online gambling. As of the time when this book was written, there were no laws prohibiting the use of credit cards and bank accounts for online gambling. Still, it's a good idea to check out government Web sites to find the most updated information.

There is no charge for transfers to and from the merchants or service providers. However, with some funding choices it can take up to three days to process your transaction, so it would behoove you to do your homework. Although NETeller is a great way to go, remember that it will still initially take time to get your account set up and operational.

Note that when you register on more than one Internet poker site, you will have to complete each site's new account forms individually. It is then important to keep good records of your finances on every site you have funded.

Avoiding Cheaters

Collusion and fraud can be a problem, but most online poker sites have collusion-detection abilities. One of the many things this detection equipment can do is look at the hand history of cards previously played by any player in any of their games to detect any patterns of behavior that would imply that he could be colluding with another player. This type of equipment can also check on their player's IP address to stop or prevent any two or more players at the same home address from playing in the same game or tournament.

Basically, online players can cheat in two ways: through collusion and through their "all-in" protection option. You may be wondering, "What's wrong with going all in?" It's wrong when players intentionally abuse the "disconnect all-in protection" option.

Question

What is meant by all-in protection?
If you are accidentally disconnected while in a hand, you will still have rights to the main pot without putting in any more chips, and a side pot will be created for any further action from the remaining players. If you have the best hand, you will get the main pot but have no claim to any money accumulated in the side pot after your disconnection.

It is almost certain that at one time or another you will find yourself disconnected, so check your account status to make sure that your all-in protection is in order. And if you do get disconnected, be sure to reset your all-in protection before you go into another online poker game.

If you repeatedly witness a player taking a "time out" at a time when it would be very advantageous for her to be all in, or in the hand, you may be playing with someone who is cheating. You should contact your site's support staff to report the number of the hand you have just played in, and the suspected player's screen name. The hand number is usually found at the top right or left corner of your computer screen. If you cannot find it, send a chat question out to your fellow opponents and someone, if not all of them, will tell you where it is. Or you can e-mail your member support service team.

When colluding partners, also know as tag teams, are experts at cheating, it can be hard to spot them during your session in an online poker game. The squeeze play, also know as whipsawing, has been around for years and is done in offline poker rooms all the time. The squeeze play is a tactic that the "locals" like to use to fleece any new blood that happens to venture into "their" offline casino poker room or card room, and take a seat at "their" table.

The mechanics of the squeeze play are quite simple. A player who acts ahead of you will either bet or raise. Then you act. After you call or raise, a player who acts behind you will then raise or re-raise your action.

When her partner is next to act, she will raise the action. This second raise made by the opponent who was initially ahead of you may be to signal the opponent to fold if you call her re-raised action.

So let's say that the opponent behind you originally re-raised with an A-J, and the opponent who acted ahead of you, who re-raised the opponent behind you, was holding Big Slick, A-K, but you are holding pocket Queens, Q-Q, so you are not going anywhere and should just call the last raise. Obviously your opponent hopes you are not holding a big pocket pair, such as A-A, K-K, Q-Q, J-J, and pre-flop both opponents are praying for that Ace to flop. You should now get the picture and understand that you are being squeezed. And hopefully the flop will contain a Queen.

Essential

Maintaining a good table image is always a good idea no matter what the situation. For example, always reply when you see in the chat box that your opponents are sending you messages like "nh," which means nice hand. A simple "tu," thank you, should suffice.

Another form of collusion is called dumping; this is when an opponent deliberately loses to his partner. Then there is signaling, which is done by signaling information to a partner with well-concealed body language or by placing chips in certain patterns on the cards. But signaling is obviously only successful in casino poker room and card room poker games. "Soft play" is another form of collusion; it is when one opponent does not bet or re-raise in a position when she would normally do so, to prevent the hand from costing her partner more money.

All of these forms of cheating are not easy to detect during any given online or offline poker game. However, they are more easily pulled off and more effective when playing casino poker room and card room poker.

When cheating in offline games, partners are able to communicate with each other by using pre-arranged signals. Among the ways they do this is with well-orchestrated chip placement around their cards and with body movements. Online players are unable to utilize cheating skills unless they just happen to be on the telephone with each other or are e-mailing each other during the hands. This is one of the reasons many people do not like playing in online tournaments, even though many online poker pros will tell you that this type of cheating is the exception rather than the rule.

One of the many pluses of online poker play is that it is easier to observe an opponent's betting patterns. This is not only a major tell, but it can clue you into the character of some of your opponents.

There are programs available for cheating online when playing poker. The Internet is filled with such sites, with claims that their programs are 100 percent safe and legal—but just the fact that the word "cheating" is involved should tell you something. And remember, if it seems too good to be true, then it probably is!

Avoiding Distractions

The term *distraction* can mean different things to many people. For example, if you tend to be a multitasker, then a distraction or two may not have much effect on your game. You are probably the type who can have a conversation with your kids and/or spouse, pay a few bills online, and play your computer hand all without skipping a beat or breaking a sweat. So for you, a distraction would probably have to be something along the lines of an earthquake.

However, if you depend more on quiet and calm to concentrate, then any outside interference could be enough to cause you to play erratically. And the only good thing about suddenly playing poorly is that, if you are usually known as a solid player, then your erratic play could throw off all the tells your opponents thought they had picked up on you.

If you are serious about not only winning but also making money, then it is important that you be as focused as you can be when playing poker in any poker game.

⚡ Alert

Many casino poker rooms and card rooms do not allow their players to talk on their cell phones while at the table, whether they are in the hand or not, or allow reading at the table, whether in a hand or not. So why would you do either of these things when you play online? If you're smart, you will take the hint and give your poker game your undivided attention, on- or offline.

There isn't a casino poker room or card room that would ever allow their players to participate in more than one poker game at a time, unlike when you play online, where you can play in several different games at the same time. However, most offline casinos and card rooms do allow their players to wear headsets so that they can hear whatever tunes soothe their souls.

When playing poker online you would be best served by playing music in the background, rather than having a television on that can easily distract you. And again, choose music that suits your personality and mood. But try not to listen to your music on the radio. Radio stations are also filled with distractions, including newsbreaks, DJ chatter, listener call-ins, and commercials.

If you have never played in a casino poker room or card room, but watch any of the many televised poker tournaments, then you should know that even when you are not in the hand you should be observing the actions of those players who are still in, because it is important to always remain observant.

Where Should You Play?

Distractions are not only visible; they can also be physical. Sure, playing while propped up on your bed sounds great, but will it also make you sleepy? Could you be so relaxed that you find yourself drifting off into daydreams, then snapping out of it, or falling asleep? Of course you could.

Question

Where is the best place to be in my house when I go to play online poker?
You should be in a quiet room, sitting upright in a chair, and seated in front of your computer, which should be sitting on a flat surface such as a table or desk.

People have been known to play online poker while sunbathing at the beach, floating on inflatable rafts in their pools, sitting in a coffee house, at the public library, while on the toilet, in the Jacuzzi, while at work, and in their cars. If you can think of a place with Internet access, then you can be sure that someone has played online poker there. Still, this doesn't mean it's a good idea to play wherever, whenever.

How Alcohol Can Affect Your Game

If you want to give your opponents a major advantage, and you are in the mood to lose all your money, come online a bit tipsy— or worse, drunk. Alcohol is a depressant, meaning that it will slow down your brain and inhibit your thought and concentration abilities. If you have just finished off a dozen bottles of beer, or have just consumed half a bottle of any other alcoholic beverage, this is not the best time to go online and play a few hands of poker. No matter how invincible you may feel, your faculties have been altered. Even when booze is being offered for free, most smart casino poker players drink bottled water.

Remember, anything that prevents you from concentrating on the game is a distraction and should be avoided. You will always make better decisions when you are not buzzed or multitasking and when your full attention is on the game at hand.

How to Detect Distracted Opponents

There are several ways of telling whether or not any of your opponents are being distracted. First, study the chat to see if anyone is talking about other poker games that he is playing. Or look to see if someone is discussing a soccer game that just happens to be on television. Immediately you should realize that these players are multitasking and therefore it should be easy to steal a few pots from them, since they are probably playing basic poker strategy poker and will be more likely to fold when faced with a raise or a re-raise. Someone who "chats" that he is babysitting or that the kids are driving him crazy is playing distracted. Don't be one of these people, and remember, it's in your best interest to use their distraction to your advantage.

Chapter 5

Limit Texas Hold'em Poker

Before you get started with any poker game, you should know the basic rules and terminology that go with it. Texas Hold'em is a great game to start with; it's a very popular poker game and you can play it both on- and offline. This chapter covers Limit Texas Hold'em; the next chapter will talk about No-Limit Texas Hold'em. Both chapters will include details about strategy and good and bad starting hands. By the end of these chapters you'll be ready to play this great game!

About Limit Texas Hold'em Poker

Make no mistake, Texas Hold'em is the most popular of all poker games and is played worldwide. However, it can also prove to be quite a deceptive game of cards to less-skilled players. Many newcomers think all it takes is a chip and a chair, and then call down every hand without taking note of their opponents' play. These players usually learn the hard way, if at all.

E ssential

Legends say that the earliest game of Texas Hold'em was probably played in Robstown, Texas, in the early 1900s. The game then supposedly migrated to Dallas around 1925, and then found its way to Las Vegas with a group of Texas gamblers and card sharks that included Doyle Brunson, Crandell Addington, and Amarillo Slim.

As in any game of poker, the objective in playing Limit Texas Hold'em is to win most of the hands by forming the best five cards out of seven. It's usually played by two to ten players and is a game where reading your opponents' hands is about the best strategic tool you can have. This is because when playing in a fixed-limit game, you are unable to raise enough to narrow the field. Therefore the players with drawing hands hang in there, all the way to the river, and draw out on you to win the pot.

A dealer button, a white disk that looks like a hockey puck, is used to represent the player in the most advantageous position at the table. She is last to act before the forced blinds, having had the opportunity to see how her opponents appear to feel about their hands. If no one raised, then the button player can assume that her opponents have weak hands and can take advantage of their positions by raising and, hopefully, causing the blinds to fold, narrowing her field of opponents.

Playing Texas Hold'em

Each hand of Texas Hold'em begins with a big blind, a small blind, and a round of betting. After the first round of betting is complete, the dealer then burns a card and puts out three community cards, called the flop, in the center of the board.

Then another round of betting begins, starting with the big blind, or the next player to the left of the dealer button who is still in the hand. The next card the dealer deals, after burning another card, is the turn card, or Fourth Street. And again, another round of betting takes place.

Ⓔ Fact

The burn card is the next card on the top of the deck that is moved onto the mucked pile of face-down cards without being shown to anyone. This is done between each round of betting to prevent anyone from being able to determine the next card to be dealt.

Figure 5.1 An example of a full, or ring, Texas Hold'em game (*Poker Room.com*)

The last card to be dealt on the board is the river card, or Fifth Street, which is the final betting round. After all betting is complete, the site's software will read the hands and award the pot to the best hand. If it is you, you will hear a pleasant chime coming from your computer.

The Deal

The deal is the same in all Texas Hold'em games. Starting with the small blind, each player is dealt two cards face-down pre-flop. However, when playing online, your two cards will appear face-up on your computer screen for only you to see. You then combine your two cards with the five community cards to make the best five-card hand. This hand can consist of your two hole cards and three of the cards on the board, one hole card and four cards on the board, or just your hole cards. Rarely, the best hand consists of just the cards on the board, also known as playing the board.

When all pre-flop betting has ceased, the dealer will burn a card and deal the three community flop cards out onto the center of the poker table for all players to use with their two hole cards. Then the betting again starts around the table.

A turn card, also called Fourth Street, is then added to the three community cards. Again the betting begins. When all betting has ended, the dealer deals the fifth, and final, community card, also known on the board as the river, or Fifth Street. When all the betting action is over, the best hand will win the pot and the computer software will automatically push the chips to the winner.

E ssential

Playing the board in Texas Hold'em is when the best five-card hand is on the board and not in any of the players' hands. All live hands will then chop, or split, the pot equally.

The Betting Structure

The betting structure in Limit Texas Hold'em consists of a fixed bet for each round of betting action. If you are playing in a $4/$8 limit game, the big blind would be $4 and the small blind $2. During pre-flop betting and betting after the flop, the bet is limited to multiples of $4. If no one has raised, the pot will reflect $4 multiplied by the number of players who called to see the flop.

However, if the next player to act wants to raise, then the bet must be, and can only be, raised in $4 increments. Now it will cost the next player $8 to call. Or if he should happen to re-raise, it will now cost everyone $12. As you can see, every raise increases the bet, or action, by an additional $4 per player in the hand.

The Blinds

The blinds are forced bets to ensure that there is money in the pot before the flop in all Texas Hold'em games. The small blind is usually half the amount of the big blind. In a $4/$8 limit Hold'em game this would mean that the big blind must put a $4 blind in the pot, while the small blind initially puts up a $2 blind. If there have been no raises by the time the action gets back around to the blinds, and the big blind checks, then it will only cost the small blind $2 to see the flop. That is, unless the small blind raises, which will then force the action to go around the table again, or until a maximum three raises have been made.

The Flop

Once everyone has had the opportunity to either fold, call, or raise the pre-flop betting action, it is then time for the dealer to deal three community cards out onto the center of the board, or table.

When playing online poker, you will not see any burning or shuffling of the cards; however, you may hear it, as some sites actually have sounds that you will learn to recognize for these various dealer actions.

 Fact

Community cards include the three cards dealt in the middle of the board for all the players to use in making their hands, as well as the turn, or Fourth Street, card and the river, or Fifth Street, card.

Starting with the first person in the hand to the left of the button, the second round of action begins with a check or a bet. The betting goes around the table, and should anyone raise, the betting will continue around the table up to a maximum three raises.

The Turn

Also called Fourth Street, the turn is the fourth card to be dealt alongside the three community flop cards. Once again, each player still in the hand has the opportunity to check, bet, or raise.

A third round of betting then takes place, beginning with the first live player to the left of the button and still in the hand.

What is meant by the term "live player"?
A live player is any player who is still eligible to win all or a portion of the pot. A live player can be all in on Fourth Street but still be eligible for the main pot. A side pot would then be formed for bets made by the remaining players in the hand.

The betting structure doubles on the turn. For example, if you are playing in a $4/$8 game, now the minimum amount you are allowed to bet is $8. However, should a player ahead of you raise, the action would become $16. If this action is re-raised, the bet would become $24. If the pot is re-raised a third and final time, the amount the next player has to call to see the river card is $32. But a player always has the option to fold.

The River

Also known as Fifth Street, the river is the fifth and final card to be dealt on the board. The betting on this round would begin at $8 with the option of three raises, bringing the total cost to see your opponents' hands to $32 should the betting be capped. However, if all but two players fold on the river, there can then be a showdown, and the amount of re-raising depends on the rules of the online or offline site where you are playing. Some places have a cap, or a maximum amount of additional raises, while other card rooms and online sites may allow raising to go on until one of the two opponents is out of chips. And of course, the winner of the hand is awarded the pot.

There is an order to the act of revealing hands after all the betting action on the river is over. It starts with the first player to the left of the button during a hand to act, and then goes around the table clockwise.

When playing in online Texas Hold'em games, the order of the showdown is not an issue, and the software handles this for you. However, when playing in offline games in casino poker rooms and card rooms, and when the dealer does not have control of the game, the order of the show can be an issue. This is because many seasoned players will call you down in the hope that you're bluffing. But if you show first, when they should have, they will quickly muck their cards without exposing their hands. This is particularly true in cases where your opponent holds one or two pairs, or a very low flush or straight, and he quickly thrusts his cards into the muck when he sees that he has lost the hand. And once any cards hit the muck there is no way it can be revealed when playing online, and never should be revealed for any reason when playing in any offline poker games.

Essential

When a round of betting has been capped, this means there are no more allowable bets. If a game has a maximum of three raises, then the third raise would be the cap on that round of betting.

However, when playing in offline games, if you were an active player in that hand, you are entitled to see any cards that were folded but did not hit the muck. After an online game all you have to do is click on your "Last Hand" option to bring up a window that shows the results of the last hand and all the active cards that were played during that hand. You can also specify in that same window any previous hands, usually up to the last fifty, to get a report on the active cards that were played during any of those hands.

Limit Texas Hold'em Hands

Knowledge of the hands in a poker game can be a great advantage to you—both in the card room and online. This section covers the best and worst starting hands to have in a Texas Hold'em game, as well as some information about trap hands and how to play them. Commit this information to memory as soon as you can; you'll definitely need it come game time.

Alert

Beware of players who are last to reveal their cards. There is a proper order to this process, and when playing online there is no problem because the software does it for you. But in offline games, it is the dealer's responsibility to ensure that cards are revealed in the proper order.

The Best Starting Hands

Following is a list of the universal best starting hands for Limit Texas Hold'em, starting with the very best hands:

- Ace-Ace (A-A)
- King-King (K-K)
- Queen-Queen (Q-Q)
- Ace-King, suited (A-Ks)
- Ace-Queen, suited (A-Qs)
- Jack-Jack (J-J)
- King-Queen, suited (K-Qs)
- Ace-Jack, suited (A-Js)
- King-Jack, suited (K-Js)
- Ace King, off-suit (A-K)
- Ace-Ten, suited (A-10s)

Obviously, the best two cards anyone can hold in their hand are pocket Aces. For a brief moment you cannot be beat and you will win more hands with these two cards than any other combination of two.

The second best hand would be pocket Kings. The only cards that can beat you before the flop are pocket Aces. Pocket Kings are a very strong starting hand. And when no Aces appear on the board, and with no other stronger hands possible—with the exception of someone holding a smaller pocket pair with a matching third card on the board giving them a set, or three of a kind—pocket Kings should win most of the time.

Always be aware of the higher cards that can beat you. When you are playing pocket Queens, there are only two over cards that can beat you: the Ace and the King. But this is a strong starting hand that you will call all the pre-flop raises to see the flop with. Just be very cautious if an Ace or King hits the flop.

An Ace-King, suited (A-Ks), also known as Big Slick, is a tricky but strong starting hand. If you're drawing for the nut flush or straight, then you have the best two cards in the deck pre-flop. However, if you don't get any help on the flop, you will want to see the turn card as inexpensively as possible. But if there is action, and you see no cards in your suit and you did not pair, then consider folding.

Ace-Queen (A-Q) is the second best drawing hand and quite playable pre-flop.

If you hold a Jack-Jack (J-J) in the hole, you are likely to win about 20 percent of the time. But the last thing you would want to see is an over card such as an Ace, King, or Queen on the flop, especially if there are several hands in the pot.

Essential

When playing pocket Kings and your pre-flop raise has been called, be wary if an Ace hits the board on the flop. Someone with an A-2 off-suit can beat you if an Ace does not appear on the turn card.

A suited King-Queen (K-Qs) is a great drawing hand, as is Ace-Jack (A-J), for the nut flush or straight. But if the flop doesn't help you with even a pair and there's action, fold this hand unless you're a glutton for punishment.

In the late positions the King-Jack suited (K-Js) is a very play-able hand if you're able to see the flop for no more than one raise. This is because when there is a lot of action before the flop, a suited

King-Jack (K-Js), or even an off-suit (K-J), can quickly begin to lose its luster.

An off-suit Ace-King (A-K), also known as Big Slick, is a little trickier than a suited Ace-King (A-Ks), because your only hope for the nut flush with off-suited cards is if four cards to your suited Ace or King hit the board by the river. And if the board does nothing to improve your hand, remember that you can always be beat with a measly pair of deuces.

 Question

What is an over card?
An over card is any card higher than what you hold in your hand. If you hold an Ace-Ten (A-10) and the flop is King-Nine-Seven (K-9-7), the Ace in your hand is the over card. If you had a Queen-Ten (Q-10), then the King on the board is the over card.

The last of the best Texas Hold'em starting hands is the suited Ace-Ten (A-10s). And if by sheer luck the King-Queen-Jack (K-Q-J) happens to fall on the board, you've got the nuts! You want to play starting cards that can give you the nuts, which is the best possible hand given what is on the board and what you have in your hand. If you have the nuts, you can't be beat.

The Worst Starting Hands

Here is a list of the worst starting hands for Texas Hold'em:

- Two-Seven (2-7)
- Two-Eight (2-8)
- Three-Seven (3-7) and Three-Eight (3-8)
- Two-Six (2-6)
- Two-Nine (2-9), Three-Nine (3-9), and Four-Nine (4-9)
- Two-Ten (2-10)
- Five-Nine (5-9)

- Four-Seven (4-7), Four-Eight (4-8), Five-Eight (5-8), and Three-Six (3-6)
- King, Queen, or Jack with a low, off-suited card (Kd-5h), (Qd-6h), (Jh-4d)
- Any Ace with a low, unsuited card (Ad-3h)

Essential

To ensure that you win as many hands as possible, initially stick with only the premium cards to see the flop with. Premium cards include Ace-Ace (A-A), King-King (K-K), Queen-Queen (Q-Q), Jack-Jack (J-J), and Ace-King, suited (A-Ks).

When dealt any of the worst starting cards, you should almost always muck them unless you are in the blinds and able to see the flop without a raise. However, if you choose to play any of these hands, you should be aware of a few things.

The Seven-Two (7-2) did not get its reputation because it's won a lot of tournaments over the years. Instead, these two cards are the worst two you can get—they can't even make a straight. This is because there are four cards between the Seven and the Two, and only the best five cards make a hand, so the best you can hope for is flopping a set, maybe even a full house. Don't bet your bankroll on it!

The Eight-Two (8-2) is the same problematic hand as the Seven-Two (7-2) but with a higher straight or flush draw possibility, making this also a definite folding hand.

The Eight-Three (8-3) and Seven-Three (7-3) starting hands are very problematic hands, and even if you do make your straight, you will probably still be beat.

The Six-Two (6-2) will only give you a straight if the Three-Four-Five (3-4-5) cards flop. Don't be surprised when someone else shows you down with the Seven-Six (7-6).

When considering playing the Nine-Two (9-2), Nine-Three (9-3), or Nine-Four (9-4), think kicker. If you flop a pair of Nines or worse, two Nines are on the board and you will have kicker problems with the Two, Three, and Four (2, 3, and 4) cards. And if any over cards are on the board, you will probably be beat by a higher pair.

⚡ Alert

The term *Hold'em* was not derived from any of the worst starting hands, so think about that before you decide which starting Hold'em cards you want to hold and which ones you should fold.

A Ten-Two (10-2) starting hand is another marginal hand. The best thing it has going for it is the Ten (10). So if the Ace-King-Queen-Jack (A-K-Q-J) are on the board, you, probably along with another player or two, will have the nut straight.

When considering playing a Nine-Five (9-5), know that in the long run it's a loser.

And know that the Seven-Four (7-4), Eight-Four (8-4), Eight-Five (8-5), and Six-Three (6-3) also will rarely win a pot. Only play them if you are in one of the blinds and can see the flop without a raise.

Playing a face card, or paint, with an unsuited card is a common mistake made by many amateur players. Even if a King is on the board, you'll have kicker problems and will only win if your opponent has a worse kicker.

And then there is that prized Ace with any low unsuited card. Do not give much value to an unsuited Ace with a bad kicker. Although it might hold up once in a while, and you see televised tournament players always raising with an Ace-Anything, if there are any raises ahead of you, then at the very least you are probably out-kicked.

Trap Hands and How to Play Them

Sometimes starting hands that initially appear to be very strong can lose their value quickly as you observe the action around the table. These types of hands usually contain two face cards, K-Q-J, or an A-Anything, and most inexperienced players with these cards will call raises before the flop.

E Fact

The Ten-Two (10-2), also known as Ten-Deuce, hand was immortalized when Doyle Brunson won two World Series of Poker tournament bracelets with it.

You know you're trapped when you have a piece of the board but feel that you're beat with the turn and/or the river card yet to come. And you probably are trapped if you're up against more than one opponent. The most common trap hands are listed here:

- Ace-Ten (A-10)
- Ace-Jack (A-J)
- King-Queen (K-Q)
- King-Jack (K-J)
- King-Ten (K-10)
- Queen-Jack (Q-J)
- Queen-Ten (Q-10)

When you're limping in with a trap hand and someone raises, you can easily find yourself up against one or more of the best Hold'em starting hands. But in late position, preferably the button position, trap hands can be playable, maybe even a raising hand, depending on the action ahead of you.

Let's Play Some Texas Hold'em

It's important to note that only 20 percent of all online and offline poker players will be winners 80 percent of the time. Therefore, you should only be playing in about 20 percent of the hands dealt. The tighter you play, the less you will lose and the better it will be for your long-term profits and for maintaining a healthy bankroll.

Take a look at the following examples of hands and think about what you would do when faced with the same cards and situations.

E ssential

Premium Starting Hands and How to Play Them Pre-Flop

When you only see 20 percent of the flops, you will find that you are playing very tight, and usually with only premium starting hands. Take a look at a few premium starting hands and see how they should be played pre-flop:

- A-A, K-K, Q-Q, J-J, and A-Ks should always be raised before the flop no matter what your seat position.
- 10-10, A-K, A-Qs, A-Js, and K-Qs should always call any pre-flop bets.
- A-Q, 9-9, A-10s, K-Js, Q-Js, K-10s, 8-8, A-J, K-Q, Q-10s, A-9s, J-Ts, A-8s, K-J, 7-7, Q-J, K-10, Q-10, J-10, A-7s, K-9s, Q-9s, 10-9s, and J-9s should be played only in a late position with strongly exercised judgment that can be made after watching the action around the table.

Playing Pairs

You are dealt an As-7s. The flop is Ad-7h-8s. How would you play your cards? You have flopped two pair, but not the nut two pair if someone else is holding the A-8. Or worse, what if someone holds a set of Aces, Sevens, or Eights?

It is worth a bet here, maybe even a raise, depending on how well you know your opponents, to see what the other players are holding and, hopefully, to eliminate any drawing hands. Obviously you are going for the full house and hoping that another Ace or Seven will appear on the turn or river.

If everyone has been a calling station, it is worth a bet on the river with your two pair, in the hope that your opponents are playing a pair of Aces with a high kicker. A calling station is a player who usually calls the bet but will rarely raise a hand. When she does raise, you will need to reassess the value of your hand before calling her raise. However, if you've been dealt a 7-3 in the blind and a 7-J-J hits the flop, your two pair are probably no good. So if everyone checks, you check too, because the odds of one of your opponents sandbagging a Jack in this situation are very good. And if you do see a bet, don't even think about it, just fold.

 ## Question

What is the difference between set, trips, and three of a kind?
Trips is a slang term for three of a kind, also known as triplets. And *a set* is a term used to describe trips. However, *rolled-up*, which also means three cards of the same rank, is strictly a Seven-Card Stud term for being dealt three starting cards of the same rank.

Playing Trips

If your trips, also known as a set, are concealed—meaning that you hold a pair in your hand, with the third same-ranked card on the flop—you are in good shape, especially if your set is the highest ranked card on the board.

Let's say you are holding a Jd-Js. The flop is Jh-9c-6c. You would want to come out betting, raising, or re-raising to weak out and not give anyone a chance of making a straight or flush unless he pays for it. However, if you're holding a Qh-Js and the flop is Jd-Jc-9h, bet with caution; if someone holds pocket 9-9 or, even worse, J-9, you are dead in the water unless your Q appears on the turn or the river.

But no matter what, you will usually see either one of these three-of-a-kind hands all the way to the river, then decide whether you think you're the one holding the winning hand based on your keen observation and note-taking skills. If you feel there's a possibility you can be beat, especially if you have not filled up or have the lowest full house, you might want to consider checking the river to prevent getting caught up in a check-raise situation.

Playing Straights

Ideally, you want to hold high connectors in the hole and flop the three cards that make your nut straight. At the very least you hope to catch a straight on the turn. This is especially true if the flop is flushy and you are not holding any cards of that suit.

E ssential

A straight is any five sequential cards of mixed suits, such as Qs-Jh-10h-9d-8c. You can flop a straight, turn a straight, or catch your straight on the river. An Ace-high straight is the highest straight you can make.

For example, you are holding a Jd-10h and the flop is Qs-9s-2s. You hold no spades, so, depending on the action before and after, you may want to rethink getting overly excited about your hand, as there are too many ways to get beat. However, it's worth a raise on the flop when the betting structure is still cheaper, in an attempt to weed out all other calling hands. You may not be able to lose any opponents holding a set, two pair, or the hand that holds that lone suited nut Ace, but at least you're building the pot for someone. Hopefully, for you!

Also, any flop that does not contain a pair can make a straight on the turn card, with the exception of the K-8-3, K-8-2, K-7-2, and

Q-7-2 flops. It's also important to make the best possible straight, the nut straight, because the second highest straight does nothing to improve your bankroll.

If you flop four cards to the nut straight, you should bet, raise, or even re-raise, because you want to knock out the calling hand of as many opponents as possible. Hopefully, the straight that you are looking to make is open-ended, so that you'll have more outs (cards that can make your hand) than if it's a gut-shot straight, which is when you need one of the cards in the center of the straight to make your hand.

☀ Alert

When you have the idiot straight, you are holding the lowest straight on the board, even worse than having the second nut straight. If there are any bets or raises, you should fold this hand unless you're confident your opponents hold nothing higher.

Playing Flushes

Ideally, you want to hold a suited Ace with any other card in the deck. Of course, if you are looking for a straight flush or royal flush drawing potential, you will need either paint or a suited 2-3-4-5 along with your Ace to make either of these hands.

Flushes are played like straights, but with one major exception. Only thirteen cards per suit are in a deck of fifty-two cards, so if you are hoping to catch spades and you're already holding two spades in your hand, you only have eleven possible ways of making your hand, and at least three of them must hit a board that you cannot afford to see pair. How many opponents are in the hand and what cards have been mucked will determine the likelihood of your getting the spades you need.

For example, you hold an Ad-10d and the flop is Jd-9d-3s. You're sitting on the nut flush draw, so you may want to consider a bet or a raise to thin out the field. This is called betting on the come, and at this point it's a good play, because you also want to build the pot in the hope that it will be pushed to you at the river.

Playing Full Houses

A full house usually starts with a set, or two pair, on the flop, and it's the type of hand that is almost always played to the river. Because there can be more than one full house on the board, not to mention a four of a kind, always be sure that the cards you are holding, plus the community board cards, give you the best possible full house, or you may find yourself paying off the real winner on the river.

Consider that your hole cards are K-K and the flop is A-A-K. Don't get too excited, because if several other players also called all the pre-flop raises, there's a good chance that one of your opponents is playing A-K and holds the best possible full house.

E ssential

Poker is a game of skill, luck, odds, and patience, and the odds of catching four of a kind on the turn or on the river are a major-league long shot. You'll most often fill up with, hopefully, the highest possible full house.

The A-K hand in this situation has just gotten a fantasy flop, because the chances of it being beaten on the river are slim to none. However, that's not to say that someone who is holding, say, a pocket 8-8 and has hung in there calling all the raises doesn't get really lucky and catch an 8 on the turn, and then miraculously catches the case 8 on the river, and gives the long-shot hand a four of a kind.

Playing Four of a Kind

This is another one of those situations that all poker players dream of, especially when there's a lot of action and you know you can't be beat. Ideally you would want this to be concealed and not flopped outright if you hope to get any action. This is especially true when you're holding A-A and you're a made tight player.

Question

If I flop four of a kind, when should I bet?
Never bet the limit until the river. In a case such as this, you want to give your opponents as much time to catch up as possible. Then, on the river, you hope your opponents make their hands and are now in a position to not only call your bet, but also raise you, thus enabling you to re-raise them.

By flopping an Ad-10s-Ks with Ah-Ac in your hand, check to see where the drawing hands are. Realize that someone could already have a made straight, and expect to see some action on a flop such as this one. However, if there is any action on a flop that contains A-A-x, especially if there are a lot of raises before the flop, you'll be lucky to see any called bets on the flop, let alone the river. This is why it's important to check on the flop to allow your opponents a chance to draw out their full houses.

Playing Straight Flushes and Royal Flushes

Straight flushes and royal flushes are the ultimate fantasy poker hands. They play themselves. You just check and call, and hope that everyone goes all the way to the river with you, where you can raise if you feel you won't lose any callers who have yet to act.

Chapter 6

No-Limit Texas Hold'em Poker

Not everyone is cut out to play No-Limit Texas Hold'em. It takes a type of courage that not everyone possesses. Going from Limit Texas Hold'em to No-Limit Texas Hold'em is not easy if you don't feel that your instincts are mostly on target. So if you're not sure, perhaps you should stick with the limit games and the play-money games until your confidence improves.

Playing the No-Limit Game

You see poker players saying "all in" on every televised poker tournament nearly every day of the week, and many players, especially online ones, can't resist the urge and the lure of going "all in" any time and for any reason. This is especially true when playing in the play-money Texas Hold'em games. However, if you feel you have keen instincts and consider yourself an observant, note-taking player, then maybe No-Limit Texas Hold'em is the game for you.

E ssential

When you're not running good, try to restrict yourself to only playing in games where there are a couple of weak players to give you the edge. You can figure out if the action is right by observing a few hands before deciding to click yourself into the game.

On the other hand, if the thought of pushing your chips all in, especially before the flop, makes your palms sweat and your stomach churn, then stick with Limit Texas Hold'em games and work on building up your bankroll versus possibly losing it all with two little words: all in!

An Overview of No-Limit Texas Hold'em

As in any game of poker, the objective in No-Limit Texas Hold'em is to win most of the hands you play by forming the best five cards out of a total deal of seven cards, two in your hand and five community cards. No-Limit Texas Hold'em, also known as the "Cadillac of Poker," is usually played by two to ten players and is also one of the most positional of all the poker games.

 Fact

A ring game is a game where every seat at the table has an active player seated in it, versus a short-handed game where several seats are empty either due to a lack of available players or because someone has taken a break from their computer screen or stepped out of the card room. In Texas Hold'em and Omaha games, a ring game is a table of ten players. When playing Seven-Card Stud, a ring game consists of a table of eight players.

The difference between Limit Texas Hold'em and No-Limit Texas Hold'em is this: From before the flop to the river, any player can bet as much as she wants as long as that amount is no less than the amount of the big blind, or at least twice the size of the last bet, or she can go all in at any time. In Limit Texas Hold'em, you are limited to a structured, known amount per round. An example of this would be a $4/$8 game.

The Betting Structure

The betting structure in No-Limit Texas Hold'em consists of two mandatory blinds and then whatever amount a player feels is warranted, as long as the first bet is greater than the big blind, and any raises are at least twice as much as the previous bet. However, it is common to see players who don't have a clue what to bet. So here is the best philosophy in a few words: Opening your betting action at two or three times the big blind is common.

Question

How will I know if a game that I'm observing is a good game to get involved in?
This is where your observation skills will come in handy. Watch for players who play inferior hands, or players who fold when someone becomes aggressive. If you see this behavior consistently, that's the game you want to click yourself into.

If you plan to raise, it would have to be an amount twice as much as the last bet made. If you're first to act on the turn or the river, a bet one-third the size of the pot is not a bad amount to open with. Remember, it's your goal to extract as much from your opponents as possible without trapping yourself.

The betting structure is an excellent way of picking up your opponents' tells, especially in an online game where you can't see your opponents' faces. For example, try to spot the players who open consistently for the same amount of money with premium pairs versus how they bet their middle or low pairs. Many people regularly bet $50 with premium pairs and Big Slick, $25 with suited connectors, and so on. That's called a betting pattern. If you keep good notes, you'll almost always know exactly what you're facing when up against this type of player.

Let's say you're holding an 8d-8s, your opponent is holding As-Ad, and the flop is 6d-8h-2c. You flopped a set of Eights, but your opponent has flopped nothing that helps his hand. However, he raised before the flop. If you have been doing your homework, you'll know that this player probably has a high premium pair and that the flop totally missed them. If there is already a few hundred dollars in the pot from the pre-flop action, you might consider a pot-sized bet to get rid of any possible straight draws, but not lose the pocket Aces. Or you could just go all in and try to end it before your opponent gets the chance to get lucky and catch an Ace. However, if you've been taking good notes, you'll know exactly what this player will do when up against your all-in bet.

Question

What is meant by early, middle, and late position?
When you are in early position, you are one of the first to act. Middle position is just what is says, in the middle of your herd of opponents. Late position is usually the button or the seat before the button. Before the flop, the last to act are usually the big and small blind, putting them in an excellent position to raise or re-raise.

Let's look at another example. You are holding a strong flush draw. Your hand is Qs-Js and the board after the flop is As-7c-2s. You have no idea what your opponents may be holding, and the only flush draw possibility that could hurt you is the hand that contains the King of spades with any other suited card, or even an unsuited card should another spade find its way to the board on the turn or the river. In this situation, half the size of the pot is a good opening bet, because it is just enough to make anyone with a pair of Aces call but anyone without a pair to fold. And you can get an idea of just who may be holding the King of spades or has already made their King-high flush when they raise you or go all in.

The Blinds

The blinds are forced bets to ensure that there's money in the pot before the flop. The small blind is usually half the amount of the big blind. Common examples of no-limit small and big blinds are $1/$2 and $2.50/$5, but they can also be as low as pennies.

And don't be surprised when an aggressive button player puts in a huge bet, especially when just the two blinds remain in the pot, in an attempt to steal the blinds. Stealing the blinds is when a player, usually the player on the button, raises or even goes all in to force the blinds to fold, which is usually the case unless presented with high-value cards. It's times like these when you hope to have starting premium cards so you can then kick up the button's raise or call an all-in bet.

No-Limit Texas Hold'em Hands

In this section you'll find lists of the universal best and worst starting hands for No-Limit Texas Hold'em. If you are new to the game and want to avoid being caught in difficult situations, but still want the opportunity to win big pots, you will want to memorize these starting hands and remember that good players usually participate in about 20 percent of the hands dealt.

E Alert

Do not call weak starting cards when faced with a bet. It's throwing good money after bad and the sign of a rank amateur. However, it is to your advantage to be aware of this type of player and play them accordingly to supersize the pot.

The Best Starting Hands

Playing only premium cards requires discipline, and you might get tired of waiting to play a hand. But if you use the time wisely and study each move made by every potential opponent around the table, you'll be ahead of the game when you're dealt the premium cards. The best starting hands are:

- Ace-Ace (A-A)
- King-King (K-K)
- Queen-Queen (Q-Q)
- Jack-Jack (J-J)
- Ten-Ten (10-10)

- Nine-Nine (9-9)
- Eight-Eight (8-8)
- Ace-King, suited (A-Ks)
- Ace-Queen, suited (A-Ks)

Low pocket pairs, including pairs under Eight such as 7-7, 6-6, 4-4, and 2-2, are playable. And when you flop a set, they're thrilling, but be aware of other possible sets that could be higher than the one you've just made. It's not a stretch to see over cards, any cards above an Eight, on the flop.

The Worst Starting Hands

Knowing the good starting hands is easy; it's more important that you commit the worst hands, the troubling hands, to memory. Then remember to muck them every time you find them in your hand—that is, unless you are in the blinds and can see the flop on the cheap.

Question

What does it mean to see the flop on the cheap?
When you are in the blinds, you have already committed money into the pot. So when the action gets back around to you, and if there have been no raises, or a minimum raise (usually double the big blind), then it is worth a call to see a flop that is not costing you much money. Therefore, you are seeing it cheaply, or on the cheap.

The worst starting hands for No-Limit Texas Hold'em are:

- Ace-Queen (A-Q)
- Ace-Jack (A-J)
- Ace-Ten (A-10)
- King-Queen (K-Q)
- King-Jack (K-J)
- King-Ten (K-10)
- King-Nine (K-9)

- Queen-Jack (Q-J)
- Queen-Ten (Q-10)
- Queen-Nine (Q-9)

Of course, there are other hands that you should not even consider playing unless you are the big blind and can see the flop without a raise. Some of these additional bad starting hands include Q-8, J-10, and 9-8, off-suit. Small connecting cards such as 2-3, 3-4, 2-4, 3-5, 5-6, 5-7, etc., are also bad. So are any two cards that cannot make a straight or that have only a low straight potential if you do get there, like 7-2, 8-3, 9-4, 10-5, 6-2, 7-3, and 8-4.

When playing any of the worst starting hand cards (and there are other potential trash hands out there, such as an off-suit J-7), remember that even if you do miraculously make your straight, it may not be the nut straight. So if the potential for the nut straight is out there and you decide to bet, you will remember exactly why you should never have gotten involved with this hand in the first place when you get raised. Unless it's your goal to put someone else's kids through college, don't get involved with these kinds of hands.

 Question

What is meant by a pot-size bet?
A pot-size bet equals the total amount of money that has already been bet into the pot. If $200 is in the pot on the river and someone bets $200, she has made a pot-size bet.

Trap Hands and How to Play Them

Sometimes starting hands that initially appear to be very strong can lose their value quite quickly as you observe the action around the table. These types of hands usually contain two face cards, King-Queen-Jack, or an Ace-anything, and most inexperienced players will call any raise before the flop with any of these cards.

You know you are trapped when you have a piece of the board but still need to see the river to make your hand. So study your options carefully before calling to see a card that, even if it comes, doesn't guarantee that you won't still lose the hand. The most common trap hands are:

- Small connecting cards, suited or off-suit (2-3, 2-4, 3-4, 3-5, 4-5, 4-6, etc.)
- Any two cards that cannot make you a straight, or that have only a low straight or flush potential even if you do get there (2-7, 3-8, 4-9, 5-10, 2-6, 3-7, 4-8)

When you find yourself limping in with a trap hand, and someone raises—or worse, goes all in—there is only one safe move you can make: Fold before you talk yourself into playing just to see the flop. But if you do call, and do happen to win the pot, you'll be glad when your opponents see this lousy hand, which will confuse the impression that they've formed about you. Playing this type of hand is not a good move for your bankroll but an excellent move for your table image.

Essential

You should always have respect for the strong, tight players in your game. At the very least, make note of how they play and when they raise. Then proceed with caution.

Let's Play Some No-Limit Texas Hold'em

The most common mistakes made by inexperienced no-limit players are when they play too many starting hands, call raises with weak starting hands, and don't raise their hands pre-flop when holding premium cards. Many inexperienced players will also either overbet or underbet the pot, which can put them at risk of either winning only small pots or not protecting their hands when they warrant protection.

Check out the scenarios in this section to get a feel for what you would do when faced with them. Study how the following premium pocket cards are played pre-flop, so that you will have a good idea of how to play them when you find them in your hand.

Playing Pairs

The best two pairs you hope to find in your hand in any Texas Hold'em game are the A-A and K-K. You might want to limp in with them in an early position, but you should raise if there has been any action.

When you are playing any other pairs, it takes a lot of guts to call a huge raise or all-in bet with low pocket pairs against a tight player, so always be alert. However, if you call and hit your hand on the flop, it will be a powerful, well-concealed hand.

Playing Trips

If you are the first to act and you hold a concealed pair in your hand and one card on the flop, then a bet the size of the pot is a good start. However, should an all-in bet follow and there are no made hands on the board, then you will be calling the all-in bet.

Playing Flushes and Straights

Ideally you want to be holding two high connectors and then see three cards that make either your flush or your straight on the board. What you don't want to see on the flop is a pair of anything. Nor would you want to see the board pair on the turn or the river.

But if you should pair either of your cards, and the other card is a good kicker, then you may still have a playable hand.

Playing a Full House

Your object here is to get as many drawing hands and smaller full houses as possible to stay in "your" pot, so don't scare them off by doing something as foolish as going all in on the flop. But if the devil makes you do it, and someone goes all in on top of you, all you will have to fear is a possible four of a kind, so definitely go ahead and make the call.

Question

How will I know how much to bet in an unstructured poker game?
Some schools of thought suggest that if you raise three times the size of the big blind pre-flop, and then one-third or half the size of the pot on the turn and twice the size of the pot on the river, you'll be in the right ballpark.

In other words, if you are holding an A-K and the flop is A-A-K, you know that there is absolutely nothing that can hit that board to hurt your hand. You cannot be beat—and, oh, what a wonderful feeling!

Playing Four of a Kind

This is another one of those situations that all poker players dream of, especially when there's a lot of action and you know you can't be beat. Ideally, you would want this to be a concealed hand, and not just flop it outright.

It is also better if your four of a kind is not in Aces. For some reason, most players can just smell those other two Aces in your hand. However, this usually is not as much of a problem when the lower pairs, such as 8-8, 7-7, 6-6, or 5-5, flop.

Playing Straight Flushes and Royal Flushes

Straight flushes and royal flushes are the ultimate fantasy poker hands, and they play themselves. If you want action, always try to keep your nut hand as concealed as possible until the showdown. If you have ever been told you're a good actor, now's the time for your Oscar-winning performance.

Chapter 7

Limit Omaha High-Low Poker

Omaha High-Low and High-only poker are community card games with strong starting-hand-value concepts. This means that unlike Texas Hold'em, Omaha High-Low starting hands take precedence over seat position. They are probably the second most popular online and offline choice of poker games after Texas Hold'em. This chapter will give you all the information you need to get in on an Omaha High-Low game; High-only will be covered in Chapter 8.

About Limit Omaha High-Low Poker

Limit Omaha High-Low poker is a game that uses four hole cards that should all, in some way, work together to form several possible hand combinations pre-flop. After the flop, you should see several ways of making potentially winning high and low hands, because Limit Omaha High-Low poker is a split pot game that pays players with the best low and best high hands on the board.

⚡ Alert

Your goal is to scoop the pot when you play Limit Omaha High-Low, which means that you need to have the only best low and the only best high, unless there is no low and you scoop the pot with the nut high.

Unlike when playing straight high games, with Limit Omaha High-Low you will always be presented with two options: to go high, playing hands just as you would when playing any Texas Hold'em game, or to go low, also known as Eight-or-Better. When you go low you'll want five distinct cards with no pairs and no card higher than an Eight, with the best low being A-2-3-4-5 off-suit.

As in any game of poker, the objective in Limit Omaha High-Low is to win most of the pots. You do this by using the four cards in your hand and the five community cards to make the best five-card high hand and five-card low hand and scoop the pot.

E Fact

A common mistake many Limit Omaha High-Low players make is playing too many starting hands, which is a good way to deplete your bankroll. Four cards in your hand can appear tempting to see a flop with. However this is also a game of discipline, and if you plan on succeeding more often than losing, fight the temptation to see a flop with any four hole cards.

Playing Omaha High-Low

In Limit Omaha High-Low the pot is split between the high hand and the low hand, with the players being able to use the same two cards in their hand to make either or both ends of the hand. For example, you hold As-3s-Kd-Kh and the board at the river is 10s-2c-4s-8s-Kc. You have the nut low, A-3 from your hand and the 2-4-8 from the board. And you also have the nut high flush using the same As-3s along with the 10s-4s-8s from the board.

As you can see, the same two cards can work for making both ends of the hand a scooper, unless you have to split the low end with another player who also holds an A-3. When you scoop the pot, it means that you did not have to split or chop the pot with any of the other players in the hand.

Sometimes a one-way hand can make the high and the low end of the hand. An example of this would be the A-2-3-4-5, which is the nut low, and also a straight. And if it were suited it would be not only the nut flush but also a straight flush. A-2-3-5-6 suited is another example of a nut flush hand for the high with another good low hand.

The Deal

Starting with the blinds, each player is automatically dealt four cards face-down pre-flop (but you will see your cards face-up on your computer screen). The deal is always the same when playing any limit or no-limit Omaha poker game.

You can combine your four cards with the five community cards to make the best five-card high hand and the best five-card low hand. However, unlike Texas Hold'em, with Omaha games you must use two of the four cards in your hand to win any or all of the pot.

Basically, you will want to play hands that include an A-2, A-3, or 2-3 for the low hand, along with a suited Ace for flush potential, or another high card, or a pair.

Even though you have four cards in your hand, you can use the same two cards for both your low hand and your high hand. This cannot be emphasized enough, as many beginning Omaha players have a hard time grasping this concept, along with the fact that they must use two cards from their hand, unlike only having to use one when playing Texas Hold'em.

Essential

Many beginners will chase all the way to the river with a one-way hand. Always try to play with four starting cards that give you an opportunity to get a piece of both ends of the pot if you hope to succeed in this game.

An example of this would be if you hold an Ah-2c-4d-Js and on the river the board looks like this: 4h-5h-7h-9d-10h. You have the nut low, but your best high is only a pair of Fours. That's right, a pair of Fours. Look again—you only have one heart in your hand with four hearts on the board. Remember, this isn't Texas Hold'em, and you need two hearts to make a flush when playing any Omaha games.

The Betting Structure

The betting structure is the same in any Limit Omaha game, High-Low or High-only, and consists of a fixed bet for each round of betting action. If you play in a $4/$8 limit Omaha High-Low game, the big blind would be $4 and the small blind would be $2. And during the pre-flop betting action and post-flop, the betting action would be limited to multiples of $4 if there were raises. If no one raises, the pot will reflect $4 multiplied by the number of players who called to see the flop.

On the turn and river the betting is in increments of $8. So if someone raises, it costs you $16 to call or $26 if you re-raise.

The Blinds

The blinds are forced bets to ensure that there is money in the pot before the flop and are the same for Omaha High-Low and High-only games. The small blind is usually half the amount of the big blind. In a $4/$8 Limit Omaha High-Low game, this means that the big blind must put a $4 blind in the pot, while the small blind initially puts up a $2 blind.

ɛ Alert

Seldom raise before the flop, because any Omaha game is dangerous, considering that everyone is holding four cards in their hands. After you see the flop and how it works with the cards in your hand, then make a move by raising or re-raising if you have a hand that can win if it holds up.

If there have been no raises by the time the action gets back around to the blinds, and the big blind checks, then it will only cost the small blind $2 more to see the flop. This is not the case if the small blind raises, which causes the action to go all the way around the table once again, or until the maximum three-raise limit has been made.

The Flop

Once everyone has had the opportunity to either fold, call, or raise the pre-flop betting action, it's time for the dealer to deal out three community cards in the center of the board, which is known as the flop.

There is often more raising and re-raising before the flop, when everyone thinks they're holding the best four cards. Once the flop is dealt, they may be singing a different song when they see that the board has totally missed their hand.

When playing online poker, you will not see any burning or shuffling of the cards. However, you will hear software-generated sounds that you'll learn to recognize for each action.

Starting with the first person in the hand to the left of the dealer button, the second round of action begins, which can be either a check or a bet. Again the betting action goes around the table, and should anyone raise, then the betting continues around the table until the maximum three raises have been made.

E ssential

It's often difficult to get the hang of reading the low hands when playing offline. But when playing Limit Omaha High-Low online, you don't have to worry about it because the computer software automatically reads and pays the winning hands.

Keep in mind that Limit Omaha High-Low poker is an action game, not a positional game. So expect a lot of raising and re-raising all the way to the river, because someone's always got something, even if it's a split pot low.

The Turn

Also called Fourth Street, the turn is the fourth card to be dealt alongside the three community flop cards. A third round of betting then takes place beginning with the first player to the left of the button. Once again every player remaining in the hand still has the opportunity to check, bet, or raise the play that has just preceded him.

☀ Alert

Remember, it is your aim in any Omaha High-Low games to scoop as many pots as possible, so be sure the starting hands you choose to play have several ways in which to go before you call the action to see the flop.

It is during the turn play when the betting action doubles. For example, if you are playing in a $4/$8 game, the minimum amount you are allowed to bet is $8.

However, should a player ahead of you raise the action, it will then become $16. And if this action should happen to be re-raised, the bet on the table becomes $24. But if the pot is re-raised a third and final time, then the amount to be called is $32. Of course, you always have the option to fold.

The River

Also known as Fifth Street, the river is the fifth and final card dealt on the board. The betting on this round is also a minimum of $8 with the option of three raises, bringing the total cost to see your opponents' hand to $32, if the hand is raised to the max. However, should all but two players fold on the river, then there can be a showdown, and the amount of re-raises depends on the online or offline site where you are playing. Some will have a cap, or maximum, amount of additional raises, while other card rooms and online sites may allow the re-raising process to go on until one of the two opponents is all in.

Essential

Only play hands that are capable of scooping the pot. This means you have a nut low working with your hole cards and the board cards, and at least a set of something with the turn and river cards yet to be dealt.

There is an order to the act of revealing hands after all the betting action on the river is completed. It starts with the first player to the left of the button, and then goes around the table clockwise. When playing in online Omaha High-Low games, the order of the showdown is not an issue. The game software does it for you. However, when playing in offline Omaha High-Low poker games in casinos and card rooms, and when the dealer does not have control of the table, the order of show can get to be a real issue. This is because many seasoned players will call you down in the hope that you are bluffing and that their hand, usually a pair, will beat your hand—so they want to see your cards first, even if you called to see their cards. That is what you paid for, the right to see their cards. The offline player will quickly shoot them into the muck, but the online player has no control over this. The computer software automatically reveals each hand that called the action on the river.

When offline players attempt and fail to fold their cards directly into the muck, or if the dealer takes them and places them on top of the muck and they are easily identifiable, the dealer, after the winner of the hand has been declared, can turn them over to reveal them.

This is an area where the online poker games have a real tell advantage over the offline poker games. Suppose you were heads-up with a player all the way to the river, and your opponent goes all in, and there are still better hands than yours possible, but your hand is pretty good. Deciding to fold, hoping you made the right decision, is always wise unless you are a chip burner (a person who has no respect for money). So you fold and text message your opponent asking what she had. Naturally your opponent will tell you she had the nuts. But how do you know if she's lying? Easy. After an online game is over you can click on "Last Hand" and bring up a window that shows you the result of the last hand and all the active cards that were played during that hand. You can also specify, in that same window, any previous hands, usually up to the last fifty hands dealt during that particular session of poker play, and get a report on the active cards that were played during any of those hands, too.

Question

Is there a particular type of hand that I should always fold?
Fold most hands that include a 7, 8, or 9 because they negatively impact the value of your hand, and if your straight does get there, it will probably be beat by a higher straight.

Omaha High-Low Hands

In this section you'll find lists of the universal best and worst starting hands for Omaha High-Low, as well as information on trap hands and how to play them.

The Best Starting Hands

Following is a list of the universal best starting hands for Omaha High-Low poker, starting with the best hand on down to the final hand. If you do not already know them, commit them to memory before you play in your first online or offline game of Omaha High-Low poker.

- Ace-Ace-Two-Three, double-suited (As-Ad-2s-3d)
- Ace-Ace-Two-Three, with one Ace suited (As-Ad-2s-3h)
- Ace-Ace-Two-Three, with no suited cards (As-Ad-2c-3h)
- Ace-Ace-Two-Four, double-suited (As-Ad-2s-4d)
- Ace-Ace-Two-Four, with one Ace suited (As-Ad-2s-4h)

- Ace-Ace-Two-Four, with no suited cards (As-Ad-2c-4h)
- Ace-Ace-Two-Five, double-suited (As-Ad-2s-5d)
- Ace-Ace-Two-Five, with one Ace suited (As-Ad-2s-5h)
- Ace-Two-Three-Four, preferably with an Ace suited (As-2d-3s-4c)

There are also several other types of hands that are very playable; you should at least see the flop before deciding whether to continue playing your hand. The hands would consist of A-A-2-5 suited, A-2-3-5 with a suited Ace, A-2-3-K, A-2-4-K, and A-2-5-K, all with a suited A-K, and A-2-5-Q with a suited A-Q.

Although many people feel that a hand like A-A-K-K should never be played when playing Limit Omaha High-Low, because any hand full of paint, even if suited, should be deemed unplayable, others feel that a hand like that is worth seeing a flop with because if there's no low you have a good chance of winning the pot.

E Fact

When you have a monster hand it means you are holding a very dangerous hand and that your opponents should be very careful. An example of this would be if you were holding an As-Ac-Kd-3c. The flop is Ad-Kc-2c. You have a set of Aces, a pair of Kings, and four cards to the nut club flush. And not just any club flush—you are on a royal club flush draw and the nut low draw.

When you hold As-Ad-Ks-2d and the flop is Ah-Kc-3s, you are holding a monster hand. You have a set of Aces and the best possible nut low, A-2-3-4-6. No matter what happens on the turn and the river, you know that, at the very least, you will be getting a piece of the low end of the pot and that you have a very good chance of taking the high end should you back into a flush or make your full house (if the board pairs).

The Worst Starting Hands

If you can imagine similar flops for each of the following examples, it will be easier for you to feel more confident when you begin to play Omaha High-Low online. There are many bad starting hands. Following are just a few examples that give you the gist of what not to get in the habit of playing if you want to win at this game.

- Jack-Ten-Nine-Two (J-10-9-2)
- Ace-Jack-Ten-Six (A-J-10-6)
- King-King-Queen-Queen (K-K-Q-Q)
- King-King-Jack-Jack (K-K-J-J)
- King-King-Ten-Ten (K-K-10-10)
- Queen-Queen-Jack-Jack (Q-Q-J-J)
- Queen-Queen-Ten-Ten (Q-Q-10-10)
- Jack-Jack-Ten-Ten (J-J-10-10)
- King-Queen-Jack-Two (K-Q-J-2)

Be aware of the danglers. Danglers are cards that do nothing to help your hand in any way. When you are playing in any poker game with four starting cards, you want all four of your cards to be able to form several different hands to ensure that your hand is the winner on the river.

Essential

You should never call on the flop with only a high draw when the flop shows two low cards and you haven't paired any of the high cards. Calling in the hope of something developing on the turn and the river is a quick way to financial disaster.

If you only want to play the high cards, then be sure that they are all high with no danglers. An example of a dangler hand could be Ks-Kd-Js-2c. The Deuce of clubs is the dangler. It is useless to your hand unless the flop looks like 2-2-2-x, with the x being anything, but don't count on getting that.

Trap Hands and How to Play Them

Sometimes starting hands that initially appear strong can lose their value quickly as you observe the action around the table. Such hands usually contain two face cards, K-Q-A-x, with the x being a 7, 8, 9, or 10, and most inexperienced players will call any raises before the flop with these types of hands.

You know you are trapped when you have a piece of the board but feel that you are beat. And you probably are if you are up against multiple opponents. Here are the most common trap hands:

- Two-Three-Four-Five (2-3-4-5)
- Three-Four-Five-Six (3-4-5-6)
- Seven-Six-Five-Four (7-6-5-4)
- Eight-Seven-Six-Five (8-7-6-5)
- King-Queen-Jack-Six (K-Q-J-6)
- Queen-Jack-10-5 (Q-J-10-5)
- Jack-Ten-Nine-Seven (J-10-9-7)

Now you are probably wondering, "Why is the 2-3-4-5 hand considered a trap hand?" And you're probably thinking that you'd play that hand every time it's dealt to you. So let's take a look and see why it can be a royal trap and a possible disaster. The only conceivable reason you would want to play this hand is in the hope that an Ace will flop. But what if it doesn't? What if the "flop" looks like this: K-4-5?

Now, if the Ace comes on the turn, you'll have the nut low, right? So the action begins around the table and you see a call, and a raise, and a re-raise.

Do you hang in there and take one more card off the deck just to see the turn card?

Knowing when to hold them and knowing when to fold them applies in any game of poker. So if you are willing to absorb the cost—and make no mistake about it, this hand will cost you dearly, especially if that elusive Ace never appears on the board—then by all means call, or even raise, to see if the poker gods really do hear your prayers.

 **Question**

What does it mean when a player takes one more card off?
When you take one more card off the deck, you are taking the next card, after the burn card, off the top of the deck. This is usually the turn card; however, in offline games you will hear this referred to as the river card, too. And even though you will often hear it on the turn card, if a player does not get his Ace, he will probably call all bets in the hope that he gets there on the river. Ergo, he has trapped himself.

But on the flip side, don't kill the messenger if, after you did the right thing and folded, an elusive Ace lands on the river, which would have given you a piece, if not all, of the nut low.

Only four Aces are in a deck. If there are five callers in the hand, it is safe to assume that if you do not have an Ace, and there are no Aces on the board, then four of your five callers may have an Ace in their hands. The wise course of action is to fold after the flop if you got involved in this type of hand in the first place.

Let's Play Some Limit Omaha High-Low Poker

It is important to remember that any poker game played with four cards in your hand is usually won, or lost, on the river, which is why they are called river games. So if you always make sure that you start out with four related cards that can work together to form winning hands after the flop, you will be off to a very good start.

Playing Pairs

You can play a big pair with a small pair, two small pairs, a big and medium pair, or two big pairs, but be careful; you're not playing Omaha High. Your goal here is to scoop the pot, not just win half of it.

If you're dealt A-A-2-2, A-A-3-3, or A-A-4-4 and you do not hit your set or nut low on the flop, then this type of hand becomes weaker by the minute. If you continue to play it, proceed with caution.

Alert

When you have been counterfeited, you have been duplicated. If you hold the A-2 for the nut low and the A-2 comes out on the flop and your high doesn't look very good at this point, it's time to muck your hand.

When playing any Omaha High-Low games, you want to look for a hand that will give you a possible nut high and nut low if it's your desire to scoop the pot. Two-way action hands contain cards that can give you the high and low end of the winning hands.

However, those are much better starting hands than the A-A-K-K, A-A-Q-Q, or A-A-J-J, which are all excellent Omaha High starting hands, but not desirable when you are playing a poker game where your goal is to scoop the pot.

Playing Trips

When playing trips, the more concealed your hand is, the better. Therefore, you would rather not see two same cards on the board with you holding one in your hand. This is because the minute you bet or raise, it's assumed you flopped a set, or even better, made your full house. For example, if you're playing K-K-2-3 and a Q-K-5-6 flops, you're in the driver's seat. Everyone at the table will suspect you may have an A-2-x-x, but they may not consider a set of anything else, let alone Kings. So play this hand with strength.

However, if you flop a middle set, such as Sevens, Eights, or Nines, and there are no over cards on the board, you might want to let your opponents lead the action so you don't scare off callers.

Flopping a set of low pairs—for example, Twos, Threes, Fours, or Fives—is only good when you have position. However, when you're playing A-A-x-x and you flop a set of Aces, slow play them if you feel any raise could drive out your opponents who are playing for the low end of the pot.

Playing Straights

Ideally you want connector cards in your hand. Examples of connectors would be A-2-10-J, A-3-7-8, and A-2-K-Q. When these cards are in the hole and you flop the three cards that make your nut straight, proceed with caution unless your nut straight is the best possible straight out there and there are no flush possibilities on the board.

Essential

If you are not the type to raise, then don't use flopping trips as a reason for changing your play. You'll only end up causing your opponents to fold. Maintain your non-aggressive play and then go in for the kill on the river, after your opponents think their hands are good.

Let's take a look at this example. You hold an A-3-10-J and the flop is 2-8-9. Not a bad flop. You have the nut low, A-3 potential plus the 8-9 to go with your 10-J. On the turn the board now looks like this: 2-8-9-10. Your Ten has been duplicated and anyone playing a J-Q-x-x has you beat. With one more card to come, your only chance of winning this pot is with a 4, 5, 6, or 7 to give you the nut low. But lows are quartered more frequently than highs, so if you only have a minimum invested, it's not costing you much to see the river, and you're financially ahead, then go for it, as most amateur Omaha players would. However, a savvy player may consider a fold here.

If the river disappoints with no low, but does duplicate one of your hole cards, just hope it is the Ace, giving you an Aces up final high hand but no low hand. However, be very wary of the straight potentials, as anything other than a call should tell you that your hand is beat.

Playing Flushes

Because everyone plays an Ace with any low card in Omaha High-Low, it is important, for multiple hand potentials, that your Ace be suited with another card in your hand.

However, if all four of your cards are suited, remember that there are only nine more cards to that suit left in the deck. So if you are in a ring game, rather than a short-handed game, the number of remaining suited cards that you need diminishes greatly.

Let's take a look at another hand. Your hand is As-2d-9s-4c and the flop is Ks-3s-5s. Excellent—you have flopped the nut flush and the nut low draw. But remember, when you flop the nuts it can only get worse.

E Alert

Never forget that the river is not your friend. That means if calling a raise to see the river card is going to bust your bankroll and you still only have a drawing hand, you have to ask yourself how lucky you are feeling before paying to see that final card.

On the turn the board now looks like this: Ks-3s-5s-2c. You duplicated your Two, but not to worry, your nut high hand is still solid. You should raise so you can trap all the nut low draws, and pray that nothing goes wrong on the river.

Now the river card appears and the final board is Ks-3s-5s-2c-2h. Red alert, trouble ahead, the board has paired! A paired board in any poker game is dangerous, but never as dangerous as it is in a four-card starting hand game such as Omaha High-Low and Omaha High-only.

As you can see, what started out as a nut-nut hand has ended up an expensive, worthless hand. But that's poker, and if you can't handle the many up and down swings, then perhaps you should consider taking up knitting to fill the void.

Playing Four of a Kind

This is another one of those situations that all poker players dream of, especially when there's a lot of action and you know you cannot be beat. Ideally, you would want this to be a bit concealed and not flopped outright if you hope to get any action. This is especially true when you are holding Ac-Ah-2c-2h, and especially if you are a made tight player. (A made tight player is anyone whose play is totally predictable to all his opponents, who are then able to play their hands against him accordingly.)

Take a look at this flop: As-2d-9h. You now have two sets, A-A-A and 2-2-2. There are no straight draws on the board and you have a rainbow flop, so a flush is not possible at this point. Also, there are only two cards to the low, so this is not a concern for you at this point, either.

E Fact

A rainbow board means that there is a card for each suit on the flop, with the fourth off-suit card appearing on the turn. An As-3c-6d on the flop, with a Jh on the turn, is an example of a rainbow board (As-3c-6d-Jh). Now, no matter what suited card hits the board on the river, there are no possible flushes with this type of community board cards.

If you go ahead and raise and you are a tight player, then you may scare your opponents out of the pot. Call any raises at this point, but a re-raise could end the hand if your opponents read you as a tight player.

After the turn card has been dealt, the board now looks like this: As-2d-9h-Jc. You have a set of Aces and a set of Deuces; there's no possible flush, no low, and only straight possibilities.

On the river the board now looks like this: As-2d-9h-Jc-2s. *Bingo, bango*, skyrockets go off in your head; you just made four of a kind with no low! Your opponents, who are holding a pair of Nines or Jacks in their hands, are also seeing fireworks. They just filled up, so let the betting fireworks begin!

Essential

Remember that you can only use two cards from your hand and three cards from the community board. Forgetting this—especially when you're in a raised and re-raised hand, all the way to the river with just the case Ace in your hand—can be very costly to your bankroll. This isn't Texas Hold'em, so you must use two suited cards from your hand to make your flush.

If you are the first to act, check in the hope that the full houses will start a betting war that you will gladly partake in. This is one of those times when your acting skills will come in very handy as you attempt to appear to be the underdog.

When it appears that you can't lose a hand, always let your opponents take the lead and bet, raise, and re-raise. Ideally, it will be you who gets to make the final re-raise bet. But if not, who cares? You can't lose, and with no lows it's a scooper, so let everyone else do your bidding!

Playing Straight Flushes and Royal Flushes

Straight flushes and royal flushes are the ultimate fantasy poker hands, and they play themselves. You just bet and call, and hope that everyone hangs in, all the way to the river.

An ideal example of a hand that could give you a straight flush would be Ad-4d-5h-6d. If the flop is 2d-3d-7d, you have the nut low and the nut diamond flush—and, should the turn be 2d-3d-7d-5d, you will not only have the nut low, but also two straight flushes. And you'll know that no one can have a larger one, as he would need to have the Four, which is in your hand.

What is the difference between a straight flush and a royal flush?
A royal flush is the highest straight flush possible and the highest of all ranked poker hands. It consists of five suited cards ranking from the Ace down to the Ten. A royal flush in spades would be As-Ks-Qs-Js-10s. And if it is your life's goal to one day win a huge pot with a royal flush, and you eventually make one, consider yourself lucky.

However, although straight flushes are seen more frequently when playing Omaha poker games than when playing Texas Hold'em poker games, the same does not hold true for royal flushes. The royal flush seems to be as elusive for Omaha players as it is for any other type of poker game player. To make a royal flush, two of the suited cards in your hand would have to be one of the following five cards: A-K-Q-J-10. So play for the straight flushes, as there's more potential for making them. A royal flush, although a glorious thing to behold, is a huge long shot!

Chapter 8

Limit Omaha High Poker

Limit Omaha High poker is also a community card game played mainly with the high cards. And unlike with Texas Hold'em, Omaha High starting hands take precedence over seat position at the table, based on the sheer fact that there are just a lot more playable starting hands when playing Omaha High-only poker.

 **Alert**

> The reason people tend to bust their bankroll when playing Omaha High is that they tend to play too many starting hands. And before the flop betting action in most Omaha High-only games is usually raised, re-raised, and often capped, meaning the maximum allowable bets and raises have been made.

Playing Limit Omaha High Poker

If you are not already familiar with the mechanics of an Omaha game, familiarize yourself with this four-card-in-your-hand game by reading the previous chapter. The betting structure in Limit High-Low and Limit High Omaha games is the same: a fixed bet for each round of betting action. The blinds are also the same in both types of games, with the small blind usually half of the big blind. The flop, the turn, and the river will not be discussed in this chapter, as they are the same mechanics used when playing Limit Texas Hold'em. And if you do not have a firm grasp of the mechanics used in playing the flop, turn, and river of Texas Hold'em, then you are not yet prepared to tackle the pressures of playing Limit Omaha High poker.

Omaha High poker has been called the suicide of poker, the Russian roulette of poker, and kamikaze poker, just to name a few, and the reasons for this will soon be made clear.

The difference between playing Omaha High poker versus Omaha High-Low poker is that your only goal is to make the best high hand using two cards out of your hand and three cards from the five community cards on the board. And you must use two cards from your hand and not one, as in Texas Hold'em games, in order to win the hand. The only exception would be when there are four of the same ranked card on the board, and then the kicker, the fifth card in your hand, comes into play. Hopefully you will have both the Ace and the King in your hand to ensure that you win the pot.

In Omaha High the pot is split as often as it is split in Texas Hold'em games, but not nearly as often as it is split in any of the high-low games. So obviously the cards you would want to hold should be similar to the premium cards that you would want to hold when playing Texas Hold'em, only twice as many.

E Fact

When playing Omaha High poker, the purpose of a raise is not necessarily to weed out the weak hands as much as it is a way of building huge pots. In other words, raises are pot builders, with the philosophy that any four cards before the flop can win the pot.

Because there are so many playable four-card combinations, the act of stealing the blinds, especially from the button position, is just about nonexistent when playing Limit Omaha High. This means that the maximum amount of raises allowed per round is more the rule than the exception.

Omaha High poker is definitely not a game for the timid or faint of heart, but if you like healthy pot-building games and you find that two hole cards just aren't enough, then Limit Omaha High poker just might be the game for you.

Omaha High Hands

Knowledge of the hands in a poker game will help you tremendously—both in the card room and online. This section covers the best and worst starting hands to have in an Omaha High game, as well as some information about trap hands and how to play them.

The Best Starting Hands

Following is a list of the universal best starting hands for Omaha High poker, beginning with the best playable starting hands. If you do not already know them, commit them to memory before you play in your first online or offline Omaha High poker game.

- Ace-Ace-King-King, double-suited (As-Ad-Ks-Kd)
- Ace-Ace-Queen-Queen, double-suited (As-Ad-Qs-Qd)
- Ace-Ace-Jack-Jack, double-suited (As-Ad-Js-Jd)
- Ace-Ace-Jack-Ten, double-suited (As-Ad-Js-10d)
- Ace-Ace-Ten-Ten, double-suited (As-Ad-10s-10d)
- Ace-Ace-Nine-Nine, double-suited (As-Ad-9s-9d)
- Ace-Ace-and any other 2 cards (A-A-x-x)
- Jack-Ten-Nine-Eight, double-suited (Jd-10d-9h-8h)
- King-King-Queen-Queen (K-K-Q-Q)
- King-King-Jack-Jack (K-K-J-J)

There are also many more hands, such as K-Q-J-10, K-K-10-10, K-K-A-Q, K-K-Q-J, K-K-J-10, and any other combination of four cards from the Ten to the Ace, that are very good hands to see a flop with. Double-suited connectors like Q-J-10-9, J-10-9-7, 10-9-8-7, and 9-8-7-6 are also hands worth seeing a flop with.

Remember, what you are looking for in a starting hand is at least three-way action. For example, you are dealt a Ks-Jh-Js-10d. First, you have two Jacks to work with. Then you have the second nut spade flush, the second nut straight, and two spades to the royal flush. This is a playable hand, and most Omaha players will come in with a raise when they hold hands like this one.

E ssential

When playing any limit Omaha High poker, you should be prepared to play more aggressively to maximize your wins. And being aggressive means raising and calling raises, and re-raising when you might not in a Texas Hold'em game.

The Worst Starting Hands

The worst starting hands in Limit Omaha High Poker are:

- Ace-Two-Three-Four, off-suit (As-2d-3c-4h)
- Ace-Two-Three-Five, off-suit (As-2d-3c-5h)
- Ace-Two-Three-King, off-suit (As-2d-3c-Kh)
- Ace-Two-Four-King, off-suit (As-2d-4c-Kh)
- Ace-Two-Five-King, off-suit (As-2d-5c-Kh)
- Ace-Two-Three-Queen, off-suit (As-2d-3c-Qh)
- Seven-Six-Five-Four, off-suit (7s-6c-5d-4h)
- Six-Five-Four-Three, off-suit (6s-5c-4d-3h)
- Five-Four-Three-Two, off-suit (5s-4c-3d-2h)

If you learn to steer clear of cards like these when playing Omaha High poker, then you increase your odds of coming out a winner.

And remember, this is not a game for the weak of heart. Although some players consider Omaha High poker to be more stimulating than Limit Texas Hold'em, it can also be more devastating to your bankroll. You can lose more money playing Omaha High poker than you can when playing any other type of poker. This is because you can get even in just one hand if you've been losing.

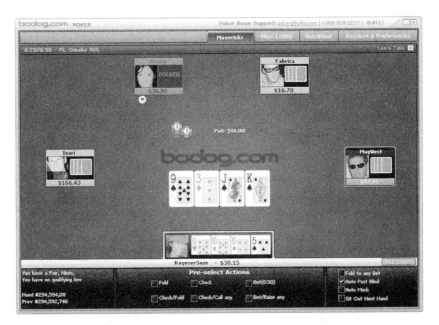

Figure 8.1 Limit Omaha High poker on Bodog.com. Even if this player gets a Queen on the river, she can still easily lose the hand to a flush or a higher straight.

 Question

How will I know what four cards to play?

Study your cards to see if you have at least three ways of making a nut hand should the right cards hit the board. Four ways to go for the nuts is an even better hand!

Trap Hands and How to Play Them

A trap hand can be any hand that initially looks good but seriously loses its value by the river card. Let's say you are dealt Qs-Qd-10d-9h and the flop is Kd-2d-5h. Your hope for flopping a three of a kind, at the very least, has just shrunk with the appearance of the King. The only worse card that could have flopped is the Ace.

Your only other realistic option, if you were to choose to remain in the pot, is a Queen-high flush, which is not normally high enough to win in an Omaha High poker hand.

E Fact

If you are dealt three of a kind and plan on playing the hand, trip Aces with a suited dangler should be the only set of trips worth seeing a cheap flop with. However, you will see many aggressive players doing this with trip Kings, too.

So a trap hand really isn't a hand you want to get involved with if your plan is to always play hands with at least three ways to go to win the pot. However, it is more important what you do after the flop because that's where you can trap yourself all the way to the river. Be careful and methodical in how you decide how many outs you have before you get yourself financially trapped in a drawing hand.

Let's Play Some Omaha High Poker

Your opponents also hold four cards in their hands. Depending on the flop, you may find yourself forced to see a hand all the way to the river and yet still lose, even though you had the winning hand all the way up to the river card. When you see the flop or the turn, this refers to, in poker-speak, the number of flops that you are willing to pay to see during any session of poker play.

And in Omaha High poker, as in any Texas Hold'em poker, you will find that the river is not your friend.

Playing Pairs

Let's say you are holding Ks-Kd-10h-9c and the flop is Kh-7d-8c. True, you have a set of Kings, but you also have an open-ended straight. On the turn the board looks like this: Kh-7d-8c-2c. You still have a three of a kind and an opened straight. But someone else may have the four to the flush, as there are now also two clubs on the board.

And then on the river the board looks like this: Kh-7d-8c-2c-6d. *Bingo*, the fairly concealed nut straight that can't be beat! And here you thought you were going to win with a set of Kings or a full house.

Playing Trips

You should never play a set of trips in your hand unless it is Aces with a suited dangler and it is relatively inexpensive for you to see a flop.

Remember: When playing trips, the more concealed your hand, the better.

Playing Straights

Let's say the flop is 9h-7d-10s and you are holding 8h-7h-Jc-Qs. You really do not want the flush to get there, unless you get perfect cards on the turn and the river, with 6h-10h hitting the board for a straight flush.

Figure 8.2 A strong Omaha High board on the turn (PokerRoom.com)

If you back into a flush with a heart on the turn and on the river, then you have kicker problems. An Eight-high flush will rarely win the day in an Omaha High poker game with more than one caller.

Playing Flushes

If you are holding As-Js-9h-8h and the flop is 10s-6s-Ks, you are not going to get many callers unless someone has flopped two pair or a set. But on the other hand, you do not want to lose your nut hand if the board should pair on the turn or the river.

E ssential

A dangler is the fourth card that doesn't work with your other three cards. If you are holding K-Q-10-2, the Deuce would be your dangler.

A raise or re-raise may be in order if there is a lot of action ahead of you. But realize that everyone will also know exactly what you have, so it is really one of those decisions that you can make only when this situation arises, because the variable from game to game will always be your opponents.

Playing Four of a Kind

This is another one of those situations that all poker players dream of. It's especially good when there is a lot of action, which there almost always is when you play any Omaha High poker, and when you know you can't be beat. Ideally, you would want this type of hand to be a bit concealed, and not flop it outright if you hope to get any real action. There will be plenty of action on the flop, but just smooth call until you see what the turn brings to your hand.

How will I know when to bet?

When you have a good hand, do not just call if you believe you have the best hand. When you believe you have the best hand, you should always bet, raise, or re-raise and not give any drawing hands a cheap chance to catch up and beat you.

Playing Straight Flushes and Royal Flushes

Straight flushes and royal flushes are the ultimate fantasy poker hands, and they play themselves. Just check or smooth call any action and then decide whether or not a raise will lose any callers at the river.

Chapter 9

Limit Seven-Card Stud Poker

Seven-Card Stud is a game of luck and skill, with the emphasis on skill. And whether you're playing Seven-Card Stud poker in a casino poker room, a professional card room, at home, or online in a virtual poker room, it's how well you have mastered the basics that will be what pays off for the solid stud-poker player in the long run. This chapter covers Limit Seven-Card Stud Poker, and Chapter 10 is all about the Seven-Card Stud High-Low game.

About Limit Seven-Card Stud Poker

Limit Seven-Card Stud is not a community card game as are Texas Hold'em and Omaha poker games. In any Seven-Card Stud poker game you have five betting rounds, whereas in Texas Hold'em and Omaha poker games, you have only four betting rounds. Each player is dealt two cards face-down and one card face-up. This is also a much slower game than the previously mentioned games, and many casinos and poker rooms offer it with antes, with the low door card bringing in the action, rather than the use of the blinds. However, many lower limit online and offline Seven-Card Stud games do not require antes, and the player with the lowest face-up card—their door card, also known as Third Street—will be forced to bet one or two dollars whether she likes her cards or not.

After the fourth card is dealt face-up on Fourth Street, the first person to act is the one with the highest showing hand on the board, and then the action continues clockwise from that player around the table.

During each round of betting the person who starts the action can change depending on each new face-up card that is dealt. (The hand with the highest face-up cards will always be the first to act after the cards are dealt for that round of betting.)

The objective of any poker game is to make the best five-card hand out of a total of seven dealt cards. Your door card is where most of your major decisions, good or bad, are made. This is because if you do not know what starting cards are playable, and you don't know what your opponents' door cards are telling you, you can find yourself beat without realizing how this could have happened. So your objective is to play three starting cards that will, hopefully, improve your hand on Fourth Street, Fifth Street, Sixth Street, and Seventh Street, this last known as the river in stud poker games.

The one most important decision you will have to make when playing Seven-Card Stud poker is whether you should play your three

Figure 9.1 A Seven-Card Stud game on the river (PokerRoom.com)

starting cards once you have seen all the door cards that have been dealt around the table.

Playing Seven-Card Stud

Seven-Card Stud poker is a five-round betting game with seven cards in a hand, two to eight players, antes instead of blinds, and a low card to bring in the action. An ante is an amount of money or chips that is put into the pot before a new game of Seven-Card Stud is dealt. This amount can be as low as fifty cents and usually increases based on the limit structures of the Seven-Card Stud game that you are playing.

 Question

What is a door card?
A door card is the third card dealt to each player. It is dealt face-up while the other two cards are dealt face-down. Your opponents' door cards let you know how many cards of a specific rank and suit have already been dealt and are therefore not available to make your hand should you need any of them.

It's important to make note of everyone's door card whether they call or fold. This is because you are getting an opportunity to see valuable cards that can either make or break your hand. You also want to be aware of how many players are in the hand and, if someone raises, what his door card is and whether he acted before or after you. You should also know whether you are in a loose game or a tight game, to give you an idea of the kind of action you can expect if you decide to raise.

Remember, when a player folds, online or offline, his door cards go into the muck with his two hole cards, so pay particular attention to each face-up card before you act or he folds.

The Deal

The deal for Seven-Card Stud games is universal and performed the same way no matter what Seven-Card Stud game you are playing.

First, starting with the player in seat one, the seat to the immediate left of the dealer button, one card at a time will be dealt around the board, with each player's first two cards being dealt face-down and their third card, the door card, being dealt face-up. On your computer screen you will see all three of your cards; however, your opponents can only see your door card, as you can only see their door cards.

These three cards are also called Third Street; this is where the player with the lowest door card (the worst possible is 2c, the Deuce of clubs) is forced to open, usually with a dollar or two. Online players don't have to do a thing with the antes or low card bets, as the computer's software automatically puts out their opening bets.

The betting action then continues clockwise, and each player, in turn, can either call, raise, or fold. If a raise takes place, then a maximum of three raises are allowed.

If you are playing in a $3 to $6 game, the low card would open for $1. There usually aren't any antes in low-limit games. This is especially true with offline poker games.

The next player can then call the $1 or raise to $3. Should there be any additional raises, they would be done in increments of $3. When the action gets back into the low card, the player who originally opened the betting for $1, she will then have the option to call the bets or to raise or re-raise.

ⒺFact

When a player "brings it in," she must place a low-limit bet into the pot to start the game's action. This can be half the size of the lowest bet allowed in any particular game, or, in some places, anywhere from $1 to $3.

A fourth card, or Fourth Street, is dealt face-up to each player starting with the first player in the hand to the left of the dealer button, and then the betting in $3 increments begins. However, on Fifth Street, when your fifth card is dealt face-up, the betting structure doubles and it will now cost $6 to bet and raise in increments of $6.

The same holds true with Sixth Street, when one more—and the last—card is dealt face-up. Again the betting, starting with the player with the highest hand on the board, starts at $6. However, on the river, Seventh Street, your final card is dealt face-down. You now have three cards face-down and four cards up, as do all your opponents.

Essential

When choosing your online action, all you have to do is review the list of moves in a readily visible action box, located at the bottom center of your computer screen, and click on your choice. Your move will be automatically performed by the computer software.

As you can see, there are a lot of cards out on the table, and many should be helping you decide how to play your hand. This is why it is so very important that you be aware of every card that has been dealt and folded face-up.

At the end of the betting, the software will read the hands and push the pot to the winner. In offline Seven-Card Stud poker games, the dealer reads the cards and pushes the pot to the winning hand.

The Betting Structure

The betting structure in Seven-Card Stud poker consists of a small opening bet made by the player dealt the lowest door card. There are many levels available online, but our examples will be based on a $3/$6 limit game. This would mean that if someone wants to raise the $1, he can raise the minimum bet to $3. However, if the bet is raised again, all subsequent raises would have to be made in $3 increments.

The betting structure would remain at $3 on Fourth Street, but on Fifth Street it is raised from $3 to $6. Now all raises will have to be made in $6 increments. On Sixth Street the betting opens at $6, as it does on Seventh Street, or the river.

When all betting has ended, the computer software will read the hands and push the pot to the winner. On most online sites you will also hear a chime sound indicating that you're a winner. In offline casino and card room games, the dealer reads the cards and pushes the pot to the winner.

Third Street

Let's say you are dealt Kd-Kh as your face-down hole cards, with a 10d as your exposed door card; you have a very good starting hand for a Limit Seven-Card Stud poker game.

⛩ Alert

Always be aware of everyone's door cards and be sure that any cards that you may need to make your hand are not already on the board.

When the betting gets around to the opening bet player, she will have the option to call an additional $2 if no one has raised. She may also call any of the raises, re-raise, or fold.

Fourth Street

In addition to your two Kings in the hole and your Ten door card, you are now dealt your second face-up card, but the fourth card to your hand. Here is how your hand now looks: face-down cards, (Kh and Ks); face-up cards, 10d and 2h. You are first to act because your hand shows the lowest ranked cards, no high card, no pairs, no sets. So you check. If anyone bets or raises, does it look as if she may be going for a straight, or that she could have a set if her door card has paired? Also make sure that there are still no Kings around the table before you decide whether or not to take one more off, and call the bet.

E Fact

When you "take one more off," you are paying to see the next card because the betting levels are still low and it is worth the call if you have a strong working hand.

And be sure to make note of any and all cards that have been folded up to this point, as they will affect not only how you continue playing your hand, but also how your opponent plays her hand. For example, it may appear that she is going for a flush, but you know that the Ace to her flush has already been folded.

Fifth Street

It is on Fifth Street where we can see hands forming and begin to get a better read on our opponents' hands. It is also on Fifth Street where the betting limits double, making it more expensive if you're still strictly on a drawing hand.

Let's say our Fifth Street hand now looks like this: (Kh-Ks)-10d-2h-Kc. But remember, on Fifth Street everyone still in the hand also has five cards. Even though you may now have a set of Kings, an opponent could have just made his straight, if that's what his exposed cards tell you, or another could have made her flush, if her exposed cards indicate a flush, or someone else could even have just filled up.

When you are not sure of a specific opponent's hand, watch for how he plays his cards. If a usually tight player suddenly bets quickly or raises, proceed with caution.

Sixth Street

By Sixth Street, if you are still on a drawing hand and the betting is getting pretty steep, you will have to make some decisions before you start throwing good money after bad. Your hand now looks like this: (Kh-Ks)-10d-2h-Kc-10h. Excellent—you fill up. Now look around the board in the hope of seeing that an opponent or two appears to have caught their flush, as they will most probably be your action.

Essential

When you make a full house on Fifth or Sixth Street, slow play your hand in the hope that a few of your opponents catch their flushes and straights on the river. Then, on the river, make your move with a raise or re-raise.

If you are first to act you might want to check here. Most Seven-Card Stud players will not automatically assume that you have made a full house here, so the nut flush hand will definitely bet, if for no other reason than to try and find out where you are with your hand. So just check or call, because you don't want to lose any players and you don't want to give your opponents any information until the river.

Seventh Street

Here is what your final hand looks like: (Kh-Ks)-10d-2h-Kc-10h-Qd. Now when you look around the board it is obvious that there are straights and flushes in your opponents' hands. If you are first to act, or in an early position, bet or call the action and hope the nut flush comes out with a raise that you will gladly re-raise when the action gets back to you. But if you see anyone with an Ace on her board with a pair, and she has called or raised all along, she may possibly have a higher full house with well-concealed Aces in the hole.

When all betting has ceased, the computer software will turn over the cards, starting with the hand that was last to act and continuing clockwise around the table from there. The software will then read the hands and award the pot to the winning hand.

Seven-Card Stud Hands

As with the other poker games you've read about so far, knowledge of hands will be a big help to you when playing Seven-Card Stud. This section covers the best and worst starting hands to have in a Seven-Card Stud game, as well as some information about trap hands and how to play them.

 Fact

Quite a few online poker rooms offer an automatic mucking option if you lost the hand and do not want your opponents to see what you were calling with. If this feature is available on the Internet site you play on, it would be wise to select this option to avoid giving away any tells.

The Best Starting Hands

Following is a list of the universal best starting hands for all Seven-Card Stud games, starting with the best hand and working down to the least of the best playable hands. All of the top five starting hands should be raised before the flop. And if you do not already know them, commit them to memory before you play in your first online or offline Seven-Card Stud poker game.

- Ace-Ace-Ace (A-A-A)
- King-King-King (K-K-K)
- Queen-Queen-Queen (Q-Q-Q)
- Jack-Jack-Jack (J-J-J)
- Ten-Ten-Ten (10-10-10)
- Ace-Ace-x, suited (As-Ad, 9s)
- King-King-x, suited (Kh-Kd-Jh)
- Queen-Queen-x, suited (Qd-Qs-8s)
- Jack-Jack-x, suited (Jh-Jd-8d)
- Ten-Ten-x, suited (10d-10h-Jd)

If you play only these starting hands, you may not play many hands—but when you do play, you will usually do well as long as you do not trap yourself and chase.

Question

What kinds of cards would make up medium pairs and connectors?
Medium pairs would be cards such as 9-9-x, 8-8-x, and 7-7-x, and your medium connectors would look something like Js-10s-x, Js-9s-x, 10d-9d-x, down to 8c-7c-x.

There are also other starting hands that many slightly looser players still consider premium starting hands. These would include starting hands with As-Qs-10s or any other high cards that give you the nut flush and a potential straight or royal flush. Many players will play any three suited cards as long as one is the Ace.

The Worst Starting Hands

Following is a list of the universal worst starting hands for Seven-Card Stud games, starting with the best of the worst, and working your way down to the last of the playable hands:

- Ace-Two-Seven, off-suit (As-2d-7c)
- Ace-Two-Eight, off-suit (As-2d-8c)
- Two-Five-Nine, off-suit (2s-5d-9c)
- Ace-Two-Five-King, off-suit (As-2d-5c-Kh)
- Ace-Two-Nine, off-suit (As-2c-9d)

The first three cards you are dealt in a Seven-Card Stud poker game will tell you whether you should fold, call, raise, or re-raise. When your cards speak to you, always listen; when you do, you will make fewer costly mistakes.

Your first three starting cards are the most important of all the cards you will be dealt. And if you do not make the right decision on Third Street, and choose to call any bets with a mediocre or bad three-card starting hand, then you will most likely end up being outdrawn and losing the hand.

So the best advice you will get regarding bad starting hands is to just not even think about playing them if you don't have any pairs or any real drawing possibilities.

E Alert

When playing Texas Hold'em games, all you have to be concerned with is how the board helps you make the nuts. You have only five cards to study, along with your hole cards, to see if your hand is the best hand out there. However, when playing Seven-Card Stud poker, you have to do this not only with your cards but also with the four face-up cards of each of your opponents to try to figure out what they could possibly have that could beat you.

Trap Hands and How to Play Them

A trap hand is really not the kind of hand that you would want to play if you plan to increase your bankroll. For example: You are dealt that coveted suited Ace, along with another suited card, but your third card is what would be considered a dangler because it is completely useless in your hand. But you call to see your Fourth Street card, and your hand is now (Ac-6d)-9c-2c. The betting round is still inexpensive, so you decide to call the bet.

On Fifth Street, your hand is (Ac-6d)-9c-2c-2s. All you have is a pair of Deuces and a club flush draw. By the time the betting gets to you, the pot has been raised. Do you call the raise and pray that you see another perfect, perfect on Sixth and Seventh Street? Or do you fold and cut your losses?

Most players will call and hope for the best. So let's assume you have called and now your cards on Sixth Street look like this: (Ac-6d)-9c-2c-2s-Jc. Now you are really trapped and will have to call to see the Seventh Street card, because if you weren't strong enough to fold on Fifth Street, then you surely won't be strong enough, let alone disciplined enough, to fold on Sixth Street.

Let's Play Some Limit Seven-Card Stud Poker

Just as you did with the other poker games, it's now time to consider some possible card scenarios. Following are the types of hands you can be dealt on Third Street and how you should play them.

Playing Pairs

There are pairs, and then there are pairs, and it is the premium pairs that you will want to play and raise with. Your premium pairs should include A-A, K-K, Q-Q, J-J, 10-10. And the last thing you want to do is limp in with premium cards and give your opponents a chance to see their Fourth Street card cheaply.

 Fact

> If you are unable to make the correct decision on Third Street and limp in with a weak starting hand, then you are sure to lose to any stronger starting hands, or, at the very least, be trapped all the way to the river.

Let's say that you didn't raise your pair of Kings. Your hand is now (Ks-Kd)-9h. After the Fourth Street card is dealt, your hand becomes (Ks-Kd)-9h-6d. Now remember, you did not raise before the flop, giving all your opponents the opportunity to limp in. So here is an example of a hand that you allowed to be limped in on, and it is usually the player who had to bring in the action with the lowest door card, (2h-7c)-2c, who is the limper. Now, on Fourth Street, the limper's hand looks like this: (2h-7c)-2c-2s. You gave an opponent the opportunity to catch a set of Deuces while you still hold only a pair of Kings.

E ssential

Then there are all those other pairs, which could be any pair from the Nines to Twos that are playable, but with restrictions. Obviously if you have a pair of Nines you would not want to see any opened cards higher than your Nine. And you definitely wouldn't want to see any exposed Nines other than your own.

If you had a choice, would you prefer your pair of Nines accompanied by an Ace kicker or a Deuce kicker? The only way a Deuce kicker is going to help you is if you see two more of them on the following streets. But don't bet your bankroll on it. And if there are any exposed over pairs on the board, dump that pair of Nines immediately.

Playing Trips

Being dealt a set of trips is a fantasy starting hand when playing Seven-Card Stud poker. When you start out with a set of trip Aces, you have no fears of being beat by a higher set. The only thing that will usually beat your Aces is when a player plays his or her three-card nut flush, or the nut straight, draw.

There are two schools of thought when it comes to playing trips. One is that you raise and do everything in your power to prevent any drawing hand from hanging in there on the cheap only to draw out on your already made hand of three of a kind.

The other school of thought goes something like this: Since trips usually win without any improvement, you should slow play them in an attempt to keep as many opponents in the hand as possible and call all the way to Seventh Street, where you can then raise the action.

For example, if you have a set of Queens and choose to slow play them, therefore allowing your opponents with higher door cards, like an Ace or a King, to limp in, don't be surprised if, at the showdown, the two hands look like these: Your hand, (Qs-Qc)-Qd-9c-3h-8s-4d, and your opponent's final hand, (9-J)-A-4-Q-10-K. That's right—your opponent not only caught your case Queen, she also backed into a straight to the Ace, beating your set of Queens. Perhaps had you put some heat on your opponent on Third and Fourth Street, you could have driven your nemesis out of the game and won a small pot instead of losing a big pot and depleting your bankroll.

 ## Question

How do I know if I should fast or slow play my set?
Although many feel that the decision to fast play trips is the proper play on Third Street, the consensus throughout the poker world seems to lean more toward a decision to slow play them if you really want to play them correctly.

Playing Straights

Three cards to a straight is simple; you want to have the best cards possible to make the best possible straight. Many people will play the middle connector cards, thinking that if no one else is going for a straight then they could quite possibly hold a hand that will earn them a huge pot on Seventh Street. But don't bet your next vacation on it.

The higher your starting cards, the higher your straight, and you want the highest of these three cards as concealed as possible in your hand.

For example, say your hole cards are (J-K)-10. By Seventh Street your hand looks like this: (J-K)-10-8-9-7-(A). Some of your opponents will think you made the lower straight, since the A-K-J are all down cards in your hand. However, when you get unsuited cards like 2-3-4,

2-3-5, 3-4-5, and so on, muck them without giving it another thought if you're smart.

Playing Flushes

Ideally, you will always want the Ace as one of your three starting cards on Third Street. Having the Ace guarantees you the best flush should there be more than one flush in your suit. And the higher your cards, the higher your flush should an opponent also have one in another suit. For example, an A-K-Q in your flush will usually guarantee your flush the winner.

ᕮ Alert

The lowest three cards to a straight that you want to play, should there be any raises on Third Street, are any three cards that can give you the nut straight hand by Seventh Street. These would be any cards between the Ten and the Ace.

The reason you should not get involved in playing medium suited cards is that they can be so easily beaten. So if there's a raise on Third Street, you should be folding. On Fourth Street, if a fourth suited card is not dealt to you but a couple of them hit your opponents' hands and you have paired none of your cards, you should dump your hand unless you want to find yourself completely trapped.

Playing Four of a Kind

This is another one of those situations that all poker players dream of. Ideally, you would want to have this type of hand as concealed as possible, and not dealt out on the board for everyone to see. An example of a well-concealed rolled-up hand could look like this: (J-J)-J. ("Rolled up" means that you have been dealt three cards of the same rank, which is the best three-card Seven-Card Stud starting hand you can hold.) Any time is a good time to get four of a kind, but if you were to get your fourth Jack on Seventh Street, dealt face-down, you will catch everyone totally off guard when your winning hand is revealed.

When you are rolled up with a three of a kind, you already have a monster hand. But when you pair your door card it's like Fourth of July, with fireworks going off in your head as you try to maintain your table image and continue to slow play your hand.

Playing Straight Flushes and Royal Flushes

Straight flushes and royal flushes are the ultimate in fantasy poker hands, and they also play themselves. You just call every bet and hope that everyone takes you all the way to Seventh Street.

However, there are exceptions, such as when you back into a small straight flush. For example, let's say that your cards are (Ad-4d)-9d. If on Fourth Street your hand becomes (Ad-4d)-9d-2d, you will obviously call any bets or raises to see the next street.

E ssential

When you bet a hand on the come, you are betting on your four cards to the nut flush, or your four cards to the nut straight, in the hope that if it gets there, you will have built a nice pot and weeded out some of the weaker drawing hands.

On Seventh Street, your hand is now (Ad-4d)-9d-2d-Kh-5d-(3d). That's right, a straight flush to the Five and relatively well concealed. Slow play your fantasy cards all the way to the river whenever you get them, and then smile when you point and click on the raise option.

Chapter 10

Limit Seven-Card Stud High-Low Split Poker

Seven-Card Stud High-Low Split poker, also known as Seven-Card Stud High-Low Split Eight-or-Better, is another split pot game with high and low hands as in Omaha High-Low Split poker.

Playing Limit Seven-Card Stud High-Low Split Poker

The basics and betting structure are the same in any Limit Seven-Card Stud poker game, so if you are not familiar with the mechanics of stud poker, then first read the section in Chapter 9 titled "About Limit Seven-Card Stud Poker" before you undertake any High-Low Split Seven-Card poker games.

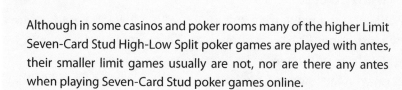

Fact

Although in some casinos and poker rooms many of the higher Limit Seven-Card Stud High-Low Split poker games are played with antes, their smaller limit games usually are not, nor are there any antes when playing Seven-Card Stud poker games online.

This is a game with a lot of twists that encourages excellent note-taking skills, a strategic mind, and patience. Your main objective is simple: to scoop the pot with the best high hand and the best low hand by starting out on Third Street with the best starting cards. So you should look for three starting cards that can lead to making the best low hand and the best high hand. You will also want to play any drawing hands as cheaply as possible. And remember, patience is a major component if you plan on winning this game.

By using five of your seven cards, you want to be able to form the best low hand and the best high hand in the game. Let's say you are holding an (As-2)-Kd. You have two cards to the nut low, two cards to the nut straight, and two cards to the nut flush. Not a bad three-card starting hand.

E ssential

Generally, when you raise, you should be prepared to pay the maximum raises to see the next street. However, if you find that the re-raises are too rich for your bankroll and find yourself folding more than calling the raises, maybe it's time to tighten up on your aggressive betting action until your luck takes a turn for the better.

Note that no pairs can exist in a low hand. A low hand is made up of the best low cards, with the highest qualifying hand for a low being 4-5-6-7-8, and the best and lowest being A-2-3-4-5.

Third Street

Ideally, you will have a suited Ace with a low card, and another low card under Five as a door card. An example of this would be (As-2s)-3h. True, there is a good chance you may have to bring in the action with the low card, but who cares with a starting hand like that? How you play your first three starting cards is extremely important, and there is great deception value when your starting hand consists of a concealed suited Ace.

Fourth Street

Sticking with the (As-2s)-3h example, now get your second card dealt face-up on Fourth Street and your hand becomes (As-2s)-3h-Js. Not bad. You have two drawing hands, one to the high end of the hand and one to the low end of the hand. But you are also in the beginning stages of getting trapped. So try to get a read on your opponents, especially if you're unsure of exactly where your opponents stand with their hands. But if someone re-raises, you might want to seriously consider your hand.

Fifth Street

A third card will be dealt face-up to each player around the table and the betting now goes up to $6 increments. Let's say your hand is now (As-2s)-3h-Js-7s. You have four cards to the nut low and four cards to the nut flush. And now you're officially trapped, because there is no way you'll be folding your hand with two more cards to come.

 Question

How do I play a made nut low on Fifth Street?
If you have the made nut low, A-2-3-4-5, on Fifth Street, you should always raise to eliminate other low draws and to prevent having to split the low portion of the pot with any of your opponents still drawing for their nut lows.

Playing Fifth Street takes a little thought and consideration. You have two separate hands to make out of your cards, and when there are several players still in the hand, that's a lot of observing, note-taking, and analysis that needs to be done in short order.

Sixth Street

Your hand now looks like this: (As-2s)-3h-J-s-7s-4d. Your low hand still remains the best, but you are still drawing for the nut flush draw.

A bet will cost $6, and as long as you have at least one way of winning the hand, bet it out and build the pot.

Question

What is meant by the term *wheel*?
A wheel is a straight to the five, and commonly a winning high hand and low hand called a scooper, in high-low split poker games.

An opponent who is obviously going for the low hand will either be aggressive to build the pot or will try to see Seventh Street as cheaply as possible in the hope of not only making his low, but also backing into a straight. That's why knowing how your opponents will act in various situations is a major advantage for you.

Seventh Street
Seventh Street is known to play itself, because if you haven't made your hand by Sixth Street, your odds of getting that perfect card greatly diminish by Seventh Street. So if there is any real action, this would be the time to fold.

Limit Seven-Card Stud High-Low Split Poker Hands
In this section you'll find lists of the universal best and worst starting hands for Limit Seven-Card Stud High-Low Split poker, as well as information on trap hands and how to play them. Commit these hands to memory before you play in your first online or offline Limit Seven-Card Stud High-Low poker game.

The Best Starting Hands
Following is a list of the universal best starting hands for Seven-Card Stud High-Low Split poker games, starting with the best hand and working down to the last of the playable hands:

- Ace-Ace with a suited Two, Three, Four, or Five (As-A-suited 2-3-4-5)
- Ace with two of the following: Two-Three-Four-Five (A-two cards under 5)
- Ace-Ace-Ace (A-A-A)
- King-King-King (K-K-K)
- Queen-Queen-Queen (Q-Q-Q)
- Jack-Jack-Jack (J-J-J)
- Ten-Ten-Ten (10-10-10)
- Nine-Nine-Nine (9-9-9)
- Ace-Ace-King, suited (Ah-Ad-Kh)
- Ace-King-King, suited (As-Ks-Kd)

If you play only these starting hands, you may not play many hands—but when you do play, you will be starting off with the best of starting hands. As long as you don't chase, you should do pretty well with them.

Ⓔ Fact

Only play three cards to the low in late position if you do not have the Ace. Otherwise, muck your cards and spend your time observing how the players who called play their cards.

Other decent starting hands would include an Ace with a pair of Queens or Jacks or Tens, with a suited kicker. And many opponents like playing their three cards to the low without any high hand cards. But even if one catches the wheel for her high hand, she probably won't be the only player in the hand.

The Worst Starting Hands

Following is a list of the universal worst starting hands for Seven-Card Stud High-Low Split poker games, starting with the best of the bad hands and moving on down to the worst playable hands:

- Deuce-Seven-Jack (2-7-J) or any other similarly spaced starting hands
- Deuce-Deuce-Seven (2-2-7)
- Three-Three-Eight (3-3-8)
- Four-Four-Nine (4-4-9)
- Five-Five-Ten (5-5-10)
- Ace-Nine-Deuce, off-suit (As-9d-2c)

If for some incredible reason you should decide to play any of these cards and you don't get a miracle flop, don't even think about it, just fold.

Your first three starting cards are the most important of all the cards you will be dealt. And if you do not make the right decisions on Third Street, and choose to stay in with mediocre or bad cards, you will almost always end up being outdrawn and will lose the hand by Seventh Street.

So the best advice regarding bad starting hands is to muck them immediately before you talk yourself into seeing a flop.

Trap Hands and How to Play Them

A trap hand is any hand that does not improve on Fourth or Fifth Street. An example of this type of hand would be (4-5)-6-K. You want the hand to go low or make a straight, but instead it appears to be going high.

E Alert

When your starting hand consists of three high suited cards, your hand must improve on Fourth Street. If it doesn't, and there is any action, you should fold unless you enjoy playing trap hands.

On Fifth Street your cards are now (4-5)-6-K-3, so you called the $3 bet. With this open-ended straight draw, you will probably also call any raises in the hope of catching your hand on Sixth Street if none of your opponents have any pairs in front of them.

Let's Play Some Limit Seven-Card Stud High-Low Split Poker

Following are the types of hands you can be dealt on Third Street and how you should play them. Ideally, you will want to see a three-way hand possibility out of your three starting cards, but as you will learn, these are not always the type of starting hands that win the pot.

Playing Pairs

There are pairs, and then there are pairs, and it is the premium pairs that you will want to play. Your premium pairs would include A-A, K-K, Q-Q, J-J, and 10-10. And if they are concealed, so much the better.

Playing Trips

When you are playing a set of anything and you allow yourself to go all the way to Sixth Street without any improvement, it is time to dump them.

 Fact

In a perfect poker world, every street would bring you another card that improves the value of your hand. But the only thing perfect about poker is when a player gets his or her perfect Sixth and Seventh Street cards and ends up winning the pot.

If you have filled up, your objective is to increase the size of the pot, not narrow the betting field, so don't overplay your hand and drive out all your opponents.

Playing Straights

You want to have the best cards possible to make the best high straight hand, and two cards that will work toward making your nut low hand. An example of this type of starting hand would be (As-Qs)-

2s. You have a nut low working, two cards to a nut flush, and two cards to a nut high. A hand like this is worth a raise in late position, even possibly a re-raise.

Playing Flushes

Ideally, you will always want the Ace as one of your three suited starting cards with at least one low card. (As-Ks)-2s is a good example of a strong low and flush starting hand.

⚡ Alert

Remember, you are playing Seven-Card Stud High-Low, so you want cards that can give you, at the very least, two-way action and not just one-way action in order to win a portion of the pot.

But if you are the type who likes going high, and your flush draw does not improve by Fifth Street, dump the hand unless you have paired your Ace or King. Playing for just a high hand is never a smart move when you are playing any High-Low poker game.

Playing Four of a Kind

This is one of those situations that all poker players dream of. You will want to have this type of hand as concealed as possible, and not dealt out on the board for everyone to see.

Playing Straight Flushes and Royal Flushes

Straight flushes and royal flushes are the ultimate in fantasy poker hands, and they also play themselves. You just bet and call, then hope that everyone takes you all the way to Seventh Street.

Chapter 11

Other Online Poker Games and Tournament Play

You now have a good foundation for the most popular poker games on the Internet, but there is still more fun to be had! This chapter is an introduction to some other great online poker games, as well as rules, tips, and strategies for playing in poker tournaments. The information you're about to read will not only help you in your online play but also applies to your experiences in offline casino poker rooms and professional card rooms.

Five-Card Draw Poker

Five-Card Draw poker is straight out of the wild, wild West and is still played today. It's easy to learn and is played similarly to Seven-Card Stud. The only obvious difference is that each player receives five cards instead of the seven cards they're dealt when playing in a Seven-Card Stud game. Five-Card Draw, however, is difficult to find online. But Planet Poker is one site that does offer this game to its online poker players.

The objective when playing in any Five-Card Draw poker game is to acquire the best five-card poker hand that you possibly can and, after the final round of betting has ended, see all the chips in the pot being pushed to you.

Some online gaming sites and casino poker and card rooms require that every player ante up before any cards are dealt. However, in the lower-limit games such as a $1/$2 limit poker game, antes are not required, but blinds are.

Just as in Texas Hold'em and Omaha poker games, the blinds rotate clockwise around the table, starting with the player to the left of the dealer button. In a $4/$8 game, the small blind would be $2 and the big blind $4.

E Fact

In Five-Card Draw poker, there are two rounds of betting. The first round is based on the five initial cards you're dealt. Each player can either call or raise in increments of $4. After the players have decided which cards in their hand they want to exchange for any or all new cards, the final betting round jumps to $8.

The Deal

The dealer deals five cards face-down to each player. You can see the faces of your own cards on your computer screen and the backs of your opponents' cards.

The first round of betting begins at $4 and can be raised three times. You'll have a list of betting options at the bottom center of your computer screen that includes fold, check, bet, check/fold, check/call any, bet/raise, and any. "Any" means you will call whatever action has been made ahead of you when it is your turn to act. The options are easily activated by a click of your mouse.

After the first round of betting, each player can discard any number of their cards, from none to all five. If you want to keep some but discard others, just click on the cards you want to hold; when it's your turn to act, you'll see them magically disappear and immediately be replaced by the next cards at the top of the deck. If you change your mind before it's your turn, simply re-click the cards to unselect them and click on the cards you want to replace.

The second round of betting begins with the first player to the left of the dealer button. Again, you have the option to fold, check, bet, check/fold, check/call any, and bet/raise. After a bet's been made, your options are limited to fold, bet, call, or raise.

After all the betting has ended, the screen will display all the hands in order and then push the pot to the player with the best hand.

Should there not be a sufficient number of cards left in the deck to complete someone's hand after they've discarded, the dealer will shuffle the discarded and mucked cards, along with the card or two left in the hand, and then complete the deal. In an offline poker room game, it's obvious and time-consuming when that happens. However, in an online game the action takes place quickly.

The Best Starting Hands

There are no set rules for the best starting hands, other than that you want to make the best five cards possible. Naturally, you want to have at the very least a high pair in your first five cards, or preferably a set of something. But ideally you want to hold a straight or a flush, or four to a drawing hand. And your fantasy first five cards would be a full house, or four of a kind. Being dealt a straight flush or a royal flush in your first five cards is a poker fantasy and rarely ever happens. If it does, remember the date and celebrate!

E ssential

Players who discard only one or none of their cards can be intimidating to all drawing-hand opponents. This is especially true if they bet or raised. This is when your good note-taking skills, knowledge, and instincts come into play.

Let's say your five down cards are As-8s-8c-Kc-9d. What would you do? Think draw poker machines; what would you hold? If you chose the A-K over a made pair, you have erred in judgment. Many will hold the 8-8 with the Ace kicker and discard two cards hoping to see another Eight or Ace.

After you receive your replacement cards, your hand could look like this: As-8s-8c-Ks-Qh. You have nothing and, hopefully, neither do your opponents, and just maybe those Eights with an Ace kicker are enough to take the pot. However, if anyone bets—or worse, raises—and you're considering calling, first ask yourself, "Am I feeling lucky today?"

The Worst Starting Hands

It's easier to muck the worst hands than it is to decide on what cards you should hold and what cards you should muck. For example, if your hand is 2-5-7-9-K, all off-suit, what would you do with it? What type of hand would you be drawing to, should you decide to play some of it? The 2-5 and the 5-7 will only get you into trouble should someone make a higher straight. The 9-K is your only option, and it's a terrible option at that. And if you think that by holding the 5-7-9 you will get a miracle 6-8 as your replacement cards, it's time to ask again if you feel lucky.

 Fact

You always want to play five cards that either complement each other or can stand alone, or cards that just need a little help. But a made hand—a high pair, two pair, a set, straight, or flush, for example—are always best when dealt in your first five cards.

When you are working on making a hand, you want to have at least three cards, preferably four cards, already working in your hand. But this hand is useless and deserves five new cards in its place.

Let's say you are dealt As-10s-9d-6s-5s. What you have is a four to the nut flush drawing hand, which is the kind of hand that you should want to play for one new card. But if you are holding 9-9-J-J-2, you would have a no-brainer. You would keep the two pair and exchange the Deuce in the hope of drawing either a Nine or a Jack.

Trap Hands

The trap hands in Five-Card Draw poker are the hands that give you three or four cards to your hand but leave you still needing one or two additional cards. Whether you are drawing to a straight or a flush, you are sometimes literally betting on one card to make your hand. So you want to see your fifth card without any raises.

E Alert

Although you can go through as many as ten cards per hand, it is not as if you are getting them all at once to pick and choose from. Being able to see seven cards, as in Texas Hold'em and Seven-Card Stud games, and nine cards, as in any Omaha game, is a distinct advantage over a five-card hand of poker where the muck and burned cards often have to be recycled into the hand.

A hand that looks like Ac-9c-4d-7c-Qd or Ad-Qh-10c-Js-9h is strictly a drawing hand. The flush has more outs, as there are more suited cards in the deck than there are individually ranked cards. For instance, the non-suited example, the nut straight draw hand, needs one of four Kings when the Nine is replaced. However, in the flush example, your draw can have as many as nine clubs still left in the deck and available to make your hand.

Either way you look at it, you are trapped, but you will always play these types of hands. Just hope that your opponent doesn't have a monster hand and that you can see your drawing cards for as cheaply as possible when you don't already have a legitimate hand.

Razz Poker

Razz is not as popular a game of poker as Texas Hold'em, Omaha, and Seven-Card Stud games, but you can find it online in a few virtual casino poker rooms and professional card rooms. It is an eight-handed poker game, dealt and played basically just like Seven-Card Stud High-Low, but played only for the low end of the hand.

The object is to have the best low possible using the Ace as a low card. The best possible hand you are looking to make is A-2-3-4-5, which is the nut low (also called a wheel). It can't be beat, only tied, and there aren't any high hands in Razz to split, so the pots will be larger than in High-Low split games.

The Deal

Razz poker is an eight-handed poker game and every player is dealt a total of seven cards, two down and one up on Third Street, with three additional cards dealt face-up on Fourth Street, Fifth Street, and Sixth Street. However, on Seventh Street your card is dealt face-down, just as it is in any Seven-Card Stud game.

To make the best five low cards, you will not want to see any paint—Kings, Queens, or Jacks—along with any Tens or Nines. And an Ace is considered a low card only, so just think of it as being the number one.

The deal and the action are exactly the same as they are in any Seven-Card Stud game. If there is an ante, the computer software will automatically subtract it from your chips and place it in the pot. Then the cards are dealt and the player with the highest card, not the lowest card as in most other games, has to bring in the action.

 Question

What does "bring in the action" mean?
When a player brings in the action it means that the person with the highest card must place a low-limit bet, whether or not he likes his cards. If it's a $3/$6 limit game, then the bring-in bet is usually $1.

Let's say your cards are (2-4)-A. The only way you would not play your cards is if your two hole cards were over a Nine. If that's not the case, these are three very good starting cards for Razz poker. And with four more cards to come, you have a good chance of improving your hand.

The betting remains at $3 until Fifth Street, when the limit is raised to $6, and there are usually three maximum raises allowed.

You should now be looking at all your opponents' door cards and counting how many low cards are already exposed on the board. Out of a deck of fifty-two cards, there are thirty-two cards that are Eight or under to keep track of.

Alert

One high card is bad enough if it is with two lows, such as A-2-K or A-3-K, but when you have two high cards, 2-Q-J, don't even think about it—muck your cards immediately. And remember, think of the Ace as the number one, and not as the highest card in the deck.

If you learn to keep track of these cards as more and more cards are revealed on the following streets, you will be in a better position to figure out whether there are enough low cards still left in the deck to warrant your calling the raises when there is only one more card to come.

By Sixth Street, your hand has become (2-4)-A-6-J-9. You have a decent low going for you but you still need one more low card, without duplicating any of the cards you already have in your hand.

Quite simply, when there is still one more card to come, and your hand still needs that one more card, you are playing a trap hand. But if you've been keeping track of the exposed cards, this hand just might be a little better than one would think.

The Best Starting Hands

Since there is no need for any card over an Eight in Razz poker, deciding on starting cards should not be difficult. If you hold no cards under the Nine in your hand, fold. If you have two high cards and one medium-low card, fold. And you don't want to see pairs and sets, even if you have a low pair with an Ace. It's hard enough to draw for two perfect cards, but to pay for the privilege of drawing three perfect cards is just not playing good poker.

Following are the premium starting-hand cards you should look for when playing Razz poker:

- Ace-Two-Three (A-2-3)
- Ace-Two-Four (A-2-4)
- Ace-Two-Five (A-2-5)
- Ace-Three-Four (A-3-4)
- Ace-Three-Five (A-3-5)
- Ace-Four-Five (A-4-5)
- Two-Three-Four (2-3-4)
- Two-Three-Five (2-3-5)

Of course there are many Razz players who will play any starting hand that contains any three low cards. But if you play tight, you will want to stick with these examples.

E Fact

If you play just high-only games and decide to check out Razz, find a play-money game online so you can practice and get the feel of working toward making a hand that you previously would have folded in a high-only game. And get used to the fact that an Ace is no greater than the number one.

The Worst Starting Hands

Since there is no such thing as a pair, set, straight, flush, or full house in Razz poker, and no card over an Eight has any value, knowing what cards you should not have in your starting hand on Third Street should be relatively simple. Any three cards that contain three high cards or two high cards and a medium-low card is a bad starting hand. If you have K-K-5, you have a bad starting hand. A-K-8 is also not a good starting hand, but there are those who will call to see a flop with this kind of hand. But this kind of starting hand, the A-K-8, will either go very well or very badly very quickly, so there is no need to see any more cards if you draw another high card on Fourth Street.

If you are rolled-up, have three of a kind, or hold a hand that in any other poker game you would usually pray for, it's useless in Razz, so you might as well muck your hand.

Trap Hands

These are the hands you shouldn't have played past Fourth Street, but, unfortunately, you didn't follow your gut instinct.

Your cards are (A-2)-J. There are three raises by the time the action gets around to you on Third Street, and you choose to call all three raises. On Fourth Street your hand now looks like this: (A-2)-J-9. True, there are still three more cards to come, and you have been keeping track of all the exposed cards and feel you have a good shot—but you should fold. However, you decide to call the raises and see your Fifth Street card.

 Question

Why am I always getting trapped?
You keep getting trapped because you play too many drawing hands all the way to Seventh Street. If you stick with the premium starting hands and make your low by or before Sixth Street, you'll cut down on the number of trap hands you tend to play.

On Fifth Street your cards are now (A-2)-J-8-5. You have four to a low, but not the nut low, so many other opponents can still beat you. You ideally need a three and a four, so if you don't see more than one of either of them on the board, you're probably thinking that you have a good chance of catching your low. So you called all the action to see Sixth Street, and this is what you now have: (A-2)-J-8-5-9. Now you are good and trapped, and probably on your way to calling the action all the way to Seventh Street.

However, at this point you should fold, because even if you do catch a fifth low card on Seventh Street, it probably won't be good enough to win the pot. But any player who has called this far will probably call all the way to the river.

Crazy Pineapple

Crazy Pineapple poker is a fun twist on Texas Hold'em poker games. The only difference is that you are initially dealt three down cards but must discard one after the flop. You then continue your play with the two remaining cards in your hand, along with the five community cards in the middle of the board, and then continue to play just as you would when playing any Texas Hold'em game. Therefore, if you are not familiar with the mechanics of Texas Hold'em, be sure to read Chapter 5 before playing in any Crazy Pineapple poker game.

Crazy Pineapple can also be played as a high-low split poker game. The only difference is that one of your three hole cards would have to be discarded after the flop. The game would then be played just like any other high-low split poker game.

E Alert

Crazy Pineapple is not a game that you should consider playing if you don't have the skills and the understanding needed to play well in any Texas Hold'em poker game. It's a fascinating game and a frustrating game and you need to possess a solid base of Hold'em knowledge if you plan on making money after you've clicked yourself into a game.

Crazy Pineapple's popularity is beginning to grow, and two Web sites currently spread the game—Paradise Poker and UltimateBet. If you prefer a site that does not offer Crazy Pineapple but you enjoy playing the game, contact your member services support team and request that they offer the game to their members.

The objective when playing Crazy Pineapple is to make the best high hand using the two remaining cards in your hand after the flop and the five community cards on the board.

The Deal

Crazy Pineapple is a ten-handed community card game played exactly like Texas Hold'em, with one exception: You are initially dealt three down cards and must discard one of these three cards right after the flop. After you have discarded the third card, you continue to play just as you would play any Texas Hold'em poker game.

 Fact

Keep in mind that when each player gets three cards before the flop—one more card than is dealt in a Texas Hold'em poker game— more cards that you might need are being dealt and mucked, and therefore may no longer be available in the deck.

The one advantage that Crazy Pineapple poker has over Texas Hold'em poker is that you initially have six cards to look at in order to help you decide what type of hand you should want to make. And just as when playing Texas Hold'em, you can use either one card from your hand and four from the community cards on the board, two cards from your hand and three community cards, or no cards from your hand when the nut hand appears on the board.

The Best Starting Hands

The following examples of starting hands are the best of the best and are usually always played by the tighter, more successful Crazy Pineapple poker players:

- Ace-Ace-King, suited (As-Ad-Ks)
- Ace-Ace-Queen, suited (As-Ad-Qd)
- Ace-Ace-Jack, suited (As-Ad-Js)

- Ace-Ace-Ten, suited (As-Ad-10d)
- King-King-Ace, suited (Ks-Kd-As)
- King-King-Queen, suited (Ks-Kd-Qs)
- King-King-Jack, suited (Ks-Kc-Js)
- King-King-Ten, suited (Ks-Kc-10s)
- Ace-Ace-with any other suited cards (As-Ah-xs)
- Queen-Queen-Ace, suited (Qs-Qc-As)

There are also many additional acceptable starting hands, like J-J-A, 10-10-A, A-K-Q, A-Q-J, and A-J-10, along with any other combination of three cards from the Ten to the Ace.

E Fact

Many poker players feel that having to post a blind is a punishment for winning the hand. But if you are a good poker player and win enough of these types of pots, you'll be more than willing to post any and all of these forced blinds.

Let's say your cards are As-9s-Js, and the flop is Ac-Ah-5s. You have three to the nut flush and a set of Aces. But you have to discard either the A-J or 9. So what will you do? You already have a made hand that is probably a winner at the moment, but you also have the nut flush drawing hand that could get there by the river if you're lucky. Always stick with the made hand. It may not get any better, but standing alone it is still a very strong poker hand.

The Worst Starting Hands

The following examples of starting hands are the best of the worst starting hands for Crazy Pineapple poker players. Two hands that appear on one line are equally bad.

- Two-Two-Seven, off-suit (2d-2c-7s)
- Two-Two-Eight (2-2-8)

- Two-Three-Seven (2-3-7) and Two-Three-Eight (2-3-8)
- Two-Six-Ten (2-6-10)
- Two-Six-Nine (2-6-9) and Two-Three-Nine (2-3-9)
- Two-Three-Ten (2-3-10)
- Two-Five-Nine (2-5-9)
- Two-Four-Seven (2-4-7) and Two-Four-Eight (2-4-8)
- Two-Five-Eight (2-5-8) and Three-Six (3-6-8)
- King, Queen, or Jack with low, off-suited cards (Kd-5h-2s), (Qd-6h-3c), (Jh-4d-2s)

As you can see, these hands are very easy to get away from before the flop. And there will be times when you do the right thing and muck them, only to see on the flop that you would have had the unbeatable nuts, or at least would have had them by the river.

Let's say you've been dealt 2h-4h-7h. You pay the price to see the flop and it shows Ah-5h-3h. You have straight flush draws and straight draws, but now you also have to pick and muck one of your cards. So do you muck the Deuce and kill one end of the straight, or muck the Seven? You decide to muck the Seven and on the turn the board now looks like this: Ah-5h-3h-7d. You mucked a Seven only to see its twin arrive on the turn.

What luck, but that's poker.

⚡ Alert

If you decide that Crazy Pineapple is the game for you and you want to continue to win, stick with the premium hands, play conservatively, and fold on the turn if your hand does not improve.

Now the river card is dealt and you see Ah-5h-3h-7d-Jh. Do you still think your Five-high flush is good enough to win the pot? Odds will dictate that someone is holding a King or a Queen, or a Ten, a Nine, an Eight, or even the Six of hearts, which is also good enough to beat your flush.

Trap Hands

As in any multi-card poker game, trap hands can be very costly in the long run when you don't get in the habit of releasing them on the turn when your hand does not improve. Therefore, any hand that you call on the turn that is still a calling hand will almost always trap you all the way to the river when you don't learn to fold on the turn.

Kill Games

Kill games are a variation on Texas Hold'em and Omaha poker games. A kill is designed to spice up a Texas Hold'em or Omaha poker game by increasing the stakes when someone has won two qualifying hands in a row. Therefore, kill games are terrific pot builders.

Question

What is the advantage to playing in games with a kill?
In one word: action. Make that three words: action, huge pots. The action pre-flop, on the flop, and on every street thereafter is always very good, especially when you are playing in any of the Omaha poker games. If you like seeing lots of action and winning huge pots, then you will love playing in kill games.

To begin with, a kill is a two-step process that can only take place after one person has won two pots in a row. Most online and offline poker rooms have a qualifying amount that must be in the pot in order for it to be considered a kill pot. For example, if there is at least $50 in both winning pots, this would qualify the next hand to be a kill in some poker rooms. In others it can be put into effect after the same person has won two pots in a row of any size. However, the amount that must be in the pot is usually calculated by multiplying the amount of the big blind times five. If you are playing in a $4/$8 limit poker game, this minimum qualifying pot size amount would be $40. Most Las Vegas poker rooms tend to round this up to $50.

Once a player has won the first qualifying pot, a "kill button" is placed in front of her. One side of this button indicates that this is a partial kill, meaning it qualifies for a full kill should this same player win the next pot. If the player does win two pots in a row, the button is flipped over to indicate that the betting structure has now increased.

As most online and offline card rooms use a half kill, the betting limits would now be $6/$12 in a $4/$8 limit game. However, if you play on- or offline and the limits go up to a full kill, the betting limits would then be $8/$16.

The Half-Kill Betting Structure

In a $6/$12 half-kill game, the winner of the kill automatically posts $6 on the kill button in front of them on the table. The big and small blinds still only have to post $2 and $4. However, anyone else who wants to call to see the flop will have to make a $6 bet.

Essential

Always remember to look over at the chat window to see if you can pick up on any of your opponents' tells. For example, you may read that two players are playing in multiple games, which tells you that their full attention is not on your game. Just knowing this can help you decide whether a raise on your fairly strong starting hand is a good move for your bankroll.

When the action returns to the two blinds, they can call the increased kill blind, raise, or fold without losing more than they would have in the blind positions. But if there have been no raises, after the two blinds call or fold, some casino poker rooms and card rooms give the last action to the player who earned the kill button; he can then either check or raise. If the kill button player chooses to raise, then the raises will be in $6 increments with a maximum of three raises. However, when playing in online poker kill games, the action goes around the table clockwise and ends with the big blind, who can then either call the additional $4, raise, or fold. And if any-one raises before the action gets back to the blinds, their raise must also be in increments of $6.

On Fifth Street the betting structure goes up to $12. So if the raises are capped on the turn and/or the river, you would have to gamble with $48 to call all the raises.

The Texas Hold'em or Omaha poker games continue as usual, with one exception: All the betting limits are increased. You're no longer playing in a $4/$8 poker game; you're now playing in a $6/$12 poker game.

Alert

Some offline casino poker rooms do not have a minimum winning pot limit in order for the kill to go into effect. As long as a player has seen a flop, even though everyone may have folded, this would be considered a first win and counted toward a kill qualifier as long as there is at least $10 in the pot.

The kill game's $6/$12 betting structure will remain at this level until another player raises to $12. If the bets are capped, it will cost you a total of $24 to see the turn card.

On the turn, the betting structure becomes $12 with a maximum of three raises, bringing your total amount to see the river card, if the betting has been capped, to $48. And it will also cost you a minimum of $12 and a maximum of $48 on the river. That is, unless you are heads-up, where the betting can be unlimited.

If the kill button player wins again, the betting structure remains at $6/$12 until someone takes the power away from the kill button player by winning the next pot.

The Full-Kill Betting Structure

Many offline casino poker rooms and card rooms offer full-kill games. When playing online you can find both half-kill and full-kill games. Make sure you know which limit kill you will be playing before you click into the game.

Full-kill poker games are played exactly like half-kill poker games with one exception: The minimum betting amounts have been doubled.

For example, a $4/$8 Texas Hold'em or Omaha poker game would now become an $8/$16 game. This means that, pre-flop and flop, the betting would be in increments of $8 and would cap the action at $32 to see the turn card. On the turn and the river, the bet is increased to $16. So if the betting action here is also capped, the cost to you, should you call, would be $64.

If you are an action junkie who loves building huge pots, then kill games may be the best betting-structure games for you.

Pot-Limit Games

Pot-Limit poker is a unique community card game played mainly with the high cards. It is a more popular poker game in Europe and online than it is in American casinos and card rooms. When looking for a pot-limit poker game online or offline, you will most often find them when you play in Omaha High poker games.

 Fact
_____

Pot-Limit Omaha poker tends to be played for higher stakes in most offline casino poker rooms and professional card rooms than when it is played in online poker rooms.

When playing in any pot-limit poker game, you will always find that your position is paramount to building your nut hand. This is mainly because if you are on a drawing hand and "pot" has been called, it will be very expensive for you to see any additional cards. However, if by chance you are holding a strong hand, you will be in a position to re-raise if, and only if, you are one of the last players to act.

Calling "pot" when playing online is very much like going "all in": It seems anti-climactic without all the grandeur and drama that are seen in live action casino or card room pot-limit poker games. That's because the online site's software does this for you after you've clicked your action. It's visually versus verbally dramatic. However, you should see *lols*, *lots of lucks*, and *gls* on the chat screen from your fellow players, usually the ones not in the hand.

E ssential

Online Internet poker sites offer their members low- and mid-level stakes Pot-Limit Omaha games. Practice in the play-money games before investing your life savings in a cash Pot-Limit Omaha game and until you feel you've perfected your game.

As in any game of poker, the objective in pot-limit poker is to win most of the hands you play by using the best five cards out of seven to form the best high hand. Showdowns are rare when playing Pot-Limit Omaha poker, but when they happen you can be certain that the two hands are most probably the nut hand and the second nut hand.

The Mechanics of a Pot-Limit Omaha High Poker Hand

To ensure that you don't make any pre-flop mistakes, remember to ask yourself if your four cards have more than three ways to make a possible nut hand. For example, if you are playing Qs-Qd-3h-8c, you are basically calling to see the flop for a Queen, as your Three and Eight are useless. This is not a good starting hand, although almost everyone will play a high pair with danglers to see the flop.

Tighten up your game by counting the options your hand has to offer before you get involved in any pot, because pot-limit games can get very expensive if you don't have any other outs, like backing into a straight or a flush. These Queens would be a much stronger hand if they looked like this: Qs-Qd-Jd-9s.

You have a potential four of a kind, full house, two straight flushes, a flush, and two straights. This is a very strong hand to see a flop with. But if you don't hit any part of your hand on the flop, and there's any action, then it has suddenly become a folding hand.

When playing Pot-Limit Omaha poker, knowing how to play your seat position and how to build your nut hands, or when to fold them, are the key factors if you plan on winning more hands than you lose.

The Betting Structure

Using a $5/$10 pot-limit betting structure, it will cost the big blind $10 and the small blind $5. Then the other eight players around the table act in turn, and at any time a player can raise, or call/click, pot. For example, if there have been five callers, including the blinds, before it's your turn to act, there would be $50 in the pot. If you called pot, you would first call the $10 and then add an additional $50 (the amount already in the pot), making your total bet $60. The pot now contains $110 and the next player to act will have to either call the $60 raise, raise it to $120, or call pot. After the flop, on the turn, and on Fifth Street and the river the betting could open at $10 and can be raised anywhere from $10 to any amount up to the pot limit.

Fact

Most bluffing in Pot-Limit Omaha poker games comes from an opponent in a later position, and she will usually try bluffing before, and right after, the flop. However, you don't see this too often on Fourth or Fifth Streets. The size of the pots, when still trying to make your drawing hand, can be healthy; the last thing a bluffer wants at that point is to be called, be raised, or hear someone call pot.

For example, on the turn we know the pot has $110 in it. So let's say your hand is Qs-Qc-10c-9s and the flop is 10s-Jc-8c. You have top pair, the Queens, four to a Queen-high flush, and an open-ended straight. Betting opens at $10 but can be raised to $120. Let's assume you are in early position, so you check the flop. The next player calls pot, and now it costs you $120 to call if everyone else calls the bet. Based on four remaining players, there is now $600 in the pot—the original $120 and the four $120 bets.

On Fourth Street, the turn, the board now looks like this: 10s-Jc-8c-Qh. You have the straight, but not the nut straight; you have a set of Queens, but you still need to fill up; and you still have four to a flush. Again someone calls pot. There is $600 in the pot; you call and the two other opponents fold. Now you are looking at an $1,800 pot.

Question

What kind of hands should I look to play when I play Pot-Limit Omaha High poker?
You want to look for hands that contain cards that coordinate well with each other. You want to see hands that can give you the nut straights, flushes, and full houses, should the flop cooperate. Always look for hands that have at least a three-way potential for flopping the nuts.

On the river the board is now 10s-Jc-8c-Qh-10c. Try to remain calm and continue to slow play your hand with a check. With any luck your opponent has also filled up . . . just hopefully not with Tens, because four Tens is the only hand that can beat you.

Your opponent calls pot; you also call, and win a $5,400 pot. Not bad for five minutes' work. But as you can see, playing in a pot-limit game calls for a much larger bankroll than when playing in limit games, and even when playing in some no-limit poker games. It is also not a game for the weak of heart, because as you saw, this game could have killed you had you not won the pot.

Remember that straight and flush drawing hands can be extremely dangerous hands to pursue when you play in any pot-limit poker games. This is because they are the ultimate trap hands, and when playing pot-limit, the last thing you want to do is find yourself financially trapped.

Tournaments

Between the televised World Series of Poker tournaments, the World Poker Tour tournaments, and the Celebrity Poker Showdown tournaments, just to name a few, the popularity of online poker has soared over the past few years. This is especially true in light of the fact that many of the people seen at the final table—and winning many of these tournaments—won their seats in an online poker tournament.

Essential

In tournament play, if the blinds are $200/$400 and you have around $2,000 in chips in front of you, a standard raise of three to four times the big blind, or $1,200 to $1,600, is appropriate and commits more than half your chips. If you are playing premium starting cards, with callers behind and in front of you, you will get decent pot odds, which is the odds of your bet compared to the amount of money in the pot, for seeing your hand all the way to the river.

A Tournament Overview

Entering an online poker tournament is as easy as finding any other game you may be interested in playing. Just click your mouse on "Tournaments," which is on the same menu window as the various games, and all available tournaments will appear on your screen.

Many sites have a preregistration for their larger tournaments and waiting lists for their members' convenience. As this differs from site to site, you may want to contact your site's member support services, and they will then e-mail you everything you need to know about the site's tournaments.

Figure 11.1 An example of a poker room tournament info screen on PokerRoom .com

 Fact

Because of the required level of skill, quick thinking, and strategizing, the overall challenge of the game, and the fact that it's aired on sports-oriented cable networks, poker is more and more becoming thought of as a sport by many.

Online poker tournaments make it possible for people all over the world to play, via the Internet, in the many play-money and real-money tournaments. These tournaments can reap you a great deal of money with little inconvenience or financial investment, and without your leaving the privacy of your own home. And there are so many tournament choices—from single-table to two-table to multi-table games, to the World Series of Poker satellites and the World Poker Tour satellites, and to the many freeroll tournaments available online daily.

E ssential

Some casino poker rooms offer their players a freeroll tournament once or twice a year. To qualify, each player must log in a certain amount of hours in a specified period of time. However, most online poker sites offer their new members a complimentary freeroll tournament seat, along with member loyalty freeroll tournaments throughout the year.

Online poker players can enter single-table tournaments, two-table tournaments, multi-table tournaments, World Series of Poker satellite tournaments, World Poker Tour tournaments, and freeroll tournaments. However, not every one of these tournaments is available on every site. Check with your member support service to request they e-mail you a complete list of all the tournaments their site offers to its members.

Now try to find a casino poker room or professional card room that offers a daily or weekly play-money tournament!

Single- and Two-Table Tournaments

Single-table and two-table tournaments are just what they sound like: one or two tables of eight to ten players. After players bust out of the game, their seats are not filled by another player, because these are what is called freeze-out tournaments. A freeze-out tournament is a tournament where each player buys in for a certain amount of money or chips and then everyone plays poker until one person has all the chips.

Usually in single- or two-table tournaments, the winner receives about half the money, while the second- and third-place players receive anywhere between 20 and 30 percent.

Figure 11.2 Freeze-out (PokerRoom.com). The player with all the chips at the end of the tournament wins.

Multi-Table and Satellite Tournaments

In multi-table online tournaments, there are usually thousands of entrants. An offline poker tournament that can come even close to that amount of entrants would be the World Series of Poker tournament.

Each player who has signed up for the online tournament is assigned a table, and as the players begin to bust out of the tournament, computer software automatically moves players around until there is only one table of players left in the tournament.

 Fact

When a player busts out of a tournament, she has gone all in and lost the hand. And with no more chips in front of her, she is eliminated from the tournament.

At this point the tournament will continue until one player holds all the chips and the game is officially over. The computer software will then divide the prize pool among the top-finishing tournament players. In multi-table tournaments, the payouts usually go to the top 5 to 10 percent of the finishers.

Satellite tournaments are a special kind of tournament where the prize is an entry into another tournament, such as The World Series of Poker or the World Poker Tour. These tournaments are signed up for ahead of time and can cost as little as nothing in a freeroll to as much as $1,000 in a buy-in satellite tournament.

Freeroll Tournaments

Most of the online poker sites offer all types of freeroll tournaments to their members. And sites including Paradise Poker, Titan Poker, and Party Poker, to name a few, offer some very exciting prizes, such as points and/or cash for entry into a larger tournament—or even better, a seat in the World Series of Poker tournament's main event.

UltimateBet has done something a little different. It offers its members a weekly freeroll tournament that would qualify them for

Figure 11.3 No one has to buy in to play in this tournament (Poker-Room.com).

a seat in a weekly televised offline tournament where the first-place winner wins $200,000 without ever having to invest a dime.

Sit-and-Go (SNG) Tournaments

A Sit-and-Go (SNG) tournament is a tournament that starts as soon as the required number of players needed for a particular game are seated around the table. However, having to wait for players is more of a problem in offline casino poker rooms and card rooms than it will ever be on Internet poker sites. There is usually so much traffic in the SNG rooms that the only waiting online, if any, is a few minutes while you wait for a table to open up.

Playing in a Sit-and-Go tournament is like being at the final table of a multi-table tournament without having to play for hours just to get there.

E ssential

Some of the more trafficked Sit-and-Go rooms can be found online in Internet poker sites including Empire Poker, Pacific Poker, Paradise Poker, Party Poker, Poker Stars, and UltimateBet.

While some sites only offer Texas Hold'em poker SNGs, other sites offer Texas Hold'em and Omaha poker SNGs. Still others offer Texas Hold'em, Omaha, and Seven-Card Stud poker SNGs.

Buy-ins can range from $1 to $1,500, with many varying buy-in limits in between, and you can get from $800 to $1,500 in player chips. The average tournament lasts about an hour, and most start off with $100/$200 blinds.

The game plays out just as it would in any poker game, with one exception: Every ten minutes the blinds go up, and this can eat you alive if you aren't an extremely tight player, but also aggressive when your hand and the game call for it.

There is a fee when you play in any real-money tournaments, and it is no different with SNGs. For example, if the buy-in is $5 and there are ten players, there should be $50 in the pot, right? That's true, but when the money is paid out to you it will be a few dollars, around $5 or $6, less. That's because the site charges $5 plus a $0.50 or $1 table fee. As the buy-ins increase, so do the fees the site charges and deducts from the buy-in money.

Re-Buy Tournaments

When playing in online poker tournaments, you'll find that most do freeze-outs versus re-buys. A freeze-out is played with the chips you received when you paid to play in the tournament. Re-buys are when you get the opportunity to "add on" to your chip stack when you are close to being all in.

⚡ Alert

Low buy-in SNGs are a good way to test your skills when you want to graduate from playing in the play-money tournaments and play in the real-money tournaments. You can start with a minimal investment if you still need a little more self-confidence.

The re-buy period of time is usually limited to the first few rounds of hands when playing in an online re-buy tournament, and within the first hour if you are playing in an offline casino poker room or card room tournament. Also, there are limited and unlimited re-buy structures. Some offline tournaments offer a one-time $100 re-buy, while others may offer unlimited re-buys of $20, provided that a player's chips have fallen below a designated amount that qualifies them for the re-buy.

At the end of the re-buy period a final add-on is usually offered to anyone in the game, and from that point on the tournament becomes a traditional freeze-out. Always take the add-on re-buy.

During the re-buy time period you will see a lot of all-ins and huge raises. However, once the re-buy period is over, this type of behavior will slow down considerably, as there's no more well to go to when an opponent runs out of chips. And players' stacks will start to dwindle quickly, with the blinds getting bigger and bigger by the minute, if they don't take any pots.

If you invest only in the initial buy-in, play tight, and then take the add-on at the end of the re-buy period, you will have invested little but will have the same opportunity to win the tournament as anyone else!

E ssential

When entering a re-buy tournament, you should always be prepared to invest in at least one re-buy. This is especially true when the re-buys are inexpensive. And when you are not sure if you should or should not invest in the re-buy, invest . . . because you are investing in yourself.

Tournament Rules, Tips, and Strategies

There are more online poker tournaments taking place at any one time than there are offline poker tournaments worldwide. Everyone now knows that a great deal of money can be won when playing online poker, and there are a lot of opportunities to qualify for some of the most prized poker tournaments in the world when you play in the low buy-in online tournaments.

It stands to reason that there would be many strategies and tips that any novice poker player should know, or be aware of, before playing in an online poker tournament.

Online Poker Tournament Rules

As in any other activity in life, following the rules is of extreme importance in the online poker world. You don't want to embarrass yourself—or, worse, lose a lot of money—by being thrown out of a poker game or kicked off a site. Following are generalized rules and standards that apply to most Internet poker sites:

- Everyone will start with the same amount of chips.
- The blinds and antes will automatically and consistently be raised throughout the tournament.
- One-table tournaments will begin within minutes after everyone is seated; however, multiple-table tournaments always have pre-set starting times and you can register one hour in advance.
- The player dealt the high card will start the tournament as the button. Should two players be dealt the same ranked card, then the suit will be the tie-breaker. For example, if two players are dealt an Ace—one gets the As, the other gets the Ad—the As is the higher ranked Ace, and the player who holds it receives the button.
- The player with all the chips at the end of the tournament is declared the winner, while players who lose all their chips are immediately eliminated from play.
- In limit poker tournaments, raises are limited to three per betting round. However, if there is a showdown between two players, the raises are usually unlimited.
- A player's blinds will automatically be posted whether he is in the hand or not.
- When a player does not act on his hand in turn, his hand will automatically be folded.
- When the tournament is down to the final two players, one player will be the big blind while the small blind also becomes the button. The small blind/button will act first before the flop and second on all action after the flop.
- Only the multi-table tournaments give breaks, ten minutes every hour. The one-on-one and Sit-and-Go tournaments do not offer any breaks.

Online Poker Tournament Tips

You've already picked up a lot of poker tips throughout this book, but there are specific tips to keep in mind when you're playing in online tournaments. Consider the following:

- Observe a few of the tournaments that you are interested in playing in and make sure to take down notes and screen names to refer back to.
- Practice in play-money tournaments as much as possible and make sure to take good notes and write down screen names. You never know who may pop into a tournament that you are playing in.
- If you play a solid game and wait for everyone else to make their mistakes and bust out, you have a much better chance of finishing in the money.
- Do not play marginal hands unless you are a blind and get to see the flop without a raise. You want to prevent taking as many hits as possible by playing solid, premium starting hands.
- When you have a superior hand, you want to get a sense of which opponents are on strong drawing hands, and therefore pot committed, and then raise in the hope of ending it right there before they draw out their cards.
- Know when you are beat when you are on a drawing hand, and know that you should fold, rather than chase.
- Save your chips for the more superior hands and fold marginal and drawing hands by Fourth Street.
- Take notes, take notes, take notes. The importance of strong observation skills and good note-taking skills cannot be emphasized strongly enough.

 Fact

When you play in multi-table tournaments you want to play as tightly and consistently as possible, allowing your opponents to knock each other out of the game. Your goal is to get to the final table, where you're usually in the money. So know what hands to play, and how to play them, and steer clear of all drawing hands.

There are many schools of thought on re-buys. Seasoned poker players don't like them, as they give players who should have been knocked out of the tournament a second chance. On the other hand, re-buys can increase the dollar value of the tournament money that will be paid out to the winners.

Online Poker Tournament Strategies

Following is basic information that all beginner and intermediate poker players should be aware of before they gamble with their savings:

- If you plan on being a successful online or offline poker player, make sure that you concentrate, are aware of your position and know how to use it to your advantage, and know what constitutes premium or strong starting hands.
- You will be more successful, and win more pots overall, when you are a disciplined, tight player.
- If you have only played in casino poker rooms and card rooms and are now going to start playing in online poker games, you will find that the online games move at a much faster pace than you are used to in offline poker games. And it's this very speed of the games that is such an allure to online poker players.
- Because of the speed of an online game, you might want to sit out a few hands and take the time to observe all the action around the table, get a read on the players, and get your bearings.
- Only deposit money in your online account that you can afford to lose.

- If you feel you are about to go on tilt, or if your strong hands are consistently losing, it's time to take a break from the poker and your computer.
- If you are preoccupied or upset about anything, it's not a good time to gamble. But if playing poker is your form of therapy, then only play in the play-money tournaments until your head has cleared.
- Always keep an eye out for any tells. Remember, you can glean some valuable information when you read the chat between your opponents.
- Take notes. This is so important that it falls under more than one category. And make sure you use the notes box on your computer screen to jot down any tells or comments about your opponents' play as often as possible.
- Don't start out in a high-limit tournament or real-money game until you have played in the lower-limit games and tournaments. This will give you time to build confidence and improve your game before being faced with some very costly decisions.

Chapter 12

Top Strategies You Should Know

All games of poker, whether Texas Hold'em, Omaha, Seven-Card Stud, or any variation of these games, have one thing in common: They are all mind games that utilize the art of bluffing and the ability to intimidate your opponents. Once you have mastered the art of good note-taking and are able to read your opponents' hands correctly, you will become a very successful poker player. This chapter focuses on bluffing and other strategies for poker success.

Various Situations and How to Play Them

When you want to mess with your opponents' heads, successfully bluff them out of a huge pot and then show your bluff. The mere showing of your cards will have a lasting effect on your opponents' play, causing them to second-guess how they'll play against you the next time. However, unless your hand goes to the river, online poker players do not have the ability to show cards.

 Fact

To help you get a read on your opponent, Party Poker, for example, has a feature that allows you to get hand histories by clicking on the hand number and requesting an e-mail history be sent to you. You usually receive these requests within minutes.

As you become more and more experienced in the online poker arena, you'll be confronted with various situations in games. The best way to be prepared for all these unknown situations is to consider as many as possible before you sit down to the poker table. That's what this section will help you do. The following examples will teach you how to play your hand if you find yourself in similar situations, using your knowledge of your opponents' styles of play.

Playing a Short Stack

Whether you play in limit, no-limit, or tournament poker games, not making adjustments in your play when you're short-stacked can be a costly mistake. Therefore, your goal is to maximize what you have left in front of you by making a few simple adjustments to your game.

E ssential

No one likes being on a short stack, especially when the poker game has a lot of action and your cards have been running more than just good. However, when the river has refused to cooperate, knowing how to make simple strategic adjustments in your play can help you improve the outcome of the hand.

In tournament and no-limit games, players on a short stack tend to look for multi-way action pots to make their stand and push in all their remaining chips. What you want to do is gradually build your stack by looking for situations where you can steal the pot from the blinds with a raise. But you should never raise your hand if you are not willing to go all the way to the river with it.

When you don't hold premium cards, but you do hold pretty good cards and you're the first player to act, this could be a good time to go all in, especially when you know that your opponents always need better than average hands to call a pre-flop raise.

Conversely, should there already be a caller or two along with the blinds in the pot, you might not want to make this move. It's your object to steal the blinds, not find yourself in a heads-up situation that can knock you out of the game or tournament.

Playing Big Slick

Whether you play them suited or unsuited, in tournaments or cash games, A-K has busted out more players because of their love affair with this combo. True, you do have a 50-50 chance of winning with them, but you also have a 50-50 chance of losing.

You can turn a 50 percent chance of winning into a 75 percent chance of winning by causing an opponent with a small pocket pair to fold in fear that you're holding an over pair, assuming he is too good a player to chase and possibly get trapped.

Following are a few pointers for getting the most out of your A-K pre-flop:

- Raise with your A-K but do not call an all-in raise with them.
- A-K loses much of its value when opponents are short-stacked and pot-committed. So don't raise when you have these types of callers, as they may have you dominated with pocket Aces or Kings. Or they could have pocket Deuces that would also have your A-K beat pre-flop.
- Realize that the size of the blinds, in relation to the size of your raise or all-in bet, has a lot to do with which pre-flop hands will call your bet. If the raise on your A-K is not greater than several times the size of the big blind, you will have callers, which is exactly what you do not want. Your object is to steal the blinds in order to build your stack, not help build your caller's stack.

Playing Heads-Up Poker

Heads-up poker, which is between two opponents only, is more about strategies than it is about your cards. So if you remember some of the following suggestions, your play should improve, as should your bankroll.

- When your opponent plays tight, raise often.
- Try to trap an overly aggressive opponent.
- Look for discrepancies in your opponent's betting patterns. Is she a calling station? Does she raise or re-raise every pot? Then use these tells to your advantage when deciding how to play your hand.
- Pay particular attention to the hands your opponents do play, and how they play their premium, middle, and low cards, and draws, before the flop.
- Never underestimate the value of a check/raise. It will slow down anyone betting on the come with a drawing hand, enabling you to see free cards when you need to in future hands.

You should never approach each opponent with the same set of eyes. Making more raises when you're in position should improve your bankroll. However, if you are up against an all-in maniac, then only call their bet if you have a monster hand.

E Alert

Playing in short-handed games is one of the most profitable forms of poker play for two reasons: The more seasoned players have the advantage over their opponents, and there are more hands dealt, which gives you more opportunities to increase your bankroll.

Playing Short-Handed

Playing short-handed can be quite profitable, but most beginners will find themselves facing an uphill battle when they try to come out ahead in short-handed games. And even though everyone gets lucky once in a while, in the long run, the more seasoned players will bankrupt the less experienced players every time.

Question

How can I play in two games at the same time?
You can use two computers with a game on each, you can switch back and forth from one game to the other on one computer, or you can reduce the screen size of both games so that you can see them both on your computer screen side-by-side.

The reason skill is so important when playing in a short-handed game is that you will be forced to play more mediocre starting hands than you would in a ring game, where there's a player in every seat, because the blinds come around more frequently. This is where good note-taking skills and knowledge of your opponents' play come in handy, and why it is so important to observe the action of a short-handed game to detect any player weaknesses before you click yourself into a seat.

Playing Multiple Tables

For good online poker players, the ability to play in multiple tables is an advantage that the offline player does not have. However, when you play in multiple games simultaneously, you should always be fully alert and have a solid grasp of the games that you play.

It is possible to play in three or more games but it is not recommended, as the concentration level that this would require is almost nonexistent. You will be prone to make errors that you would normally not make.

True, you can make twice, even three times, as much money when you are a winner playing in multiple games. But remember, no one's winning streak lasts forever.

Bluffing Works Both Ways

You know by now that bluffing is a major part of the game of poker. If you want to make some serious money, bluffing is necessary. This is true in both the casino poker room and the online arena. You need to be able to get a good read on your opponents and then take advantage of the weaker players by making a run at the pot with a stone-cold bluff. This is a positional move that, when you're last to act, gives you a major advantage over your opponents.

Semi-bluffs are a safer bet, as they are a bit less risky since you should usually have a nut flush or straight draw potential in your hand. And with two cards yet to come, you're also building the pot in the hope that your hand will get there.

There are two reasons to bluff:

- To increase your profits when you win pots without having the best hand.
- To get your opponents to call in the future when you do have the best hand.

Bluffing online does not have the same perceived value as it does in offline poker games. This is because, unless the hand goes to the river, you're unable to show your opponent your cheese hand and because many online players pay little attention and won't even pick up on your bluffing tactics. However, just knowing this puts you in the driver's seat since you are very much aware of their bluffing tactics.

The virtual world makes it easier for your opponents to try to deceive you because they don't have to look you right in the eye while attempting a bluff. And calling their bluff is just a mouse click away, causing you to call more online bluffs than you would when playing in offline poker games. So be sure to pick your bluffing hands carefully.

Pot Odds and Hand Probabilities

When you use pot odds, you are simplifying a difficult decision by turning it into a standard proposition bet. You compare how much it will cost you to call against how much is in the pot, and you can quickly see if you are getting a fair return. Pot odds are the ratio between the money already in the pot and how much it will cost you to continue to play your hand, coupled with the probability, or odds, of the strength of your hand. Therefore, if there is a 10 percent chance of winning, then there is a 90 percent chance of losing. So the odds of your losing are 9 to 1 against, meaning the odds are against you.

Knowing your probabilities is very important in helping you decide which starting cards to play and which ones to get away from. So if there is already $500 in the pot and it costs you $100 to call, you will need to know just how strong your cards are in order to decide if the amount in the pot justifies your call, or maybe even a raise.

Following are pre-flop probabilities for being dealt specific premium hands:

- A-A: 220 to 1
- K-K, Q-Q, J-J: 72.7 to 1
- 10-10, 9-9, 8-8, 7-7, 6-6: 43.2 to 1
- 5-5, 4-4, 3-3, 2-2: 54.3 to 1
- A-Ks: 331 to 1
- A-Ko: 110 to 1
- A-Qs or A-Js: 165 to 1
- A-Q or A-Jo: 54.3 to 1
- K-Qs: 331 to 1
- K-Qs: 110 to 1
- A-xs: 35.8 to 1
- A-xo: 11.3 to 1

If you have ever wondered what your odds are of holding an A-K, then flopping either an A-A-K or a K-K-A, the answer is 1,088 to 1!

Following are your probabilities for flopping specific hands:

- Four of a kind: 407 to 1
- A full house: 136 to 1
- A set: 8.3 to 1
- A flush with two suited cards: 118 to 1
- A flush draw: 8.1 to 1
- A flush draw with 2 unsuited cards: 88 to 1

Knowing your odds and probabilities can help you make the correct decision before you get involved in a hand, and that's of vital importance to maintaining a healthy bankroll. A seasoned player will know how to calculate pot odds and understand how this knowledge should be applied to their strategy to increase their profits and keep their losses at a minimum.

What to Do When You're Running Bad

Running bad can be devastating, not only to your bankroll but also to your ego. So you always need to remember that poker is a game of not only skill and patience, but also luck. Many seasoned players find themselves on losing streaks, playing many hours, days, even weeks and months, with no change. But that's the nature of poker, and you need to be able to deal with the bad times as well as the good times.

 **Question**

What should I do when I think I'm beat but could have the winner?
If you have second or third nut and the pot odds are in your favor—meaning that you can win at least three times more than what the bet will cost you—try to represent your hand as being strong and bet quickly. If you are re-raised you'll know where you stand.

Truthfully, there are some valid reasons to quit, the main ones being losing consistently over several years, not improving, and/or not enjoying yourself. You don't play poker to lose, but you don't have to give up. You can fight it. You start by asking some tough questions. Chief among them is whether you are playing just to be in action. Do you totally understand the game? Are you playing with scared money? Are you overrating your skills? Are the other players too skilled? Does it seem like other players always know your hand? Answering these questions might be the first step toward turning things around.

Every poker player goes through tough times. You will have winning streaks, but you will also have losing streaks. Following are a few tips to help soothe your soul as you go through a bad spell.

- Evaluate your game to see if there is something you should be doing or changing to improve your end results.
- Consider taking a few days or weeks off. Sometimes a time out from the game is just what you need to recharge your batteries and hone your skills.
- If you have been playing multiple tables, stop and put all your attention on one game at a time.
- Play in the play-money games for a while to give yourself time to assess your game play without it costing you a fortune.
- Observe and take notes on the games and limits you enjoy playing in to put yourself ahead of your opponents when you come up against them in the future.
- Try not to dwell on your bad beats. Figure out what you did wrong, if anything, then work at not repeating it.
- Play in lower limit games and set a daily time and dollar limit for yourself that you can stay true to.
- If you just have to play, consider the low-limit buy-in tournaments and the play-money tournaments until your game is back on track.

If you know before you start that you should never try to get back to even in any one poker session, you will be doing yourself, and your bankroll, a favor over the long run. Otherwise, you could be putting yourself at risk of going on a tilt that may be very hard to overcome. Just remember, there's always tomorrow. The more skilled you become, the more money (and fun) will flow your way.

Chapter 13

Avoiding Mistakes and Improving Your Game

There are many common poker mistakes that can happen during any online or offline poker game. Many of these mistakes are easy to correct and have little negative effect on your play when recognized and corrected. However, there are other situations that can really get you in trouble if you don't know how to recognize them when they creep into, and get in the way of, your play. Pay close attention to the information in this chapter; it will serve you well one day when you find yourself heading in the wrong direction.

Mistake: Going on Tilt

"Going on tilt" is a phrase you'll hear used all over the poker world. It originated in the pinball machine universe where players would tip or shake their machines so hard that it caused them to shut down, losing the player's game and quarter. Poker players go on tilt when they are frustrated from a really bad beat or have suffered several substantial losses. Although many online and offline players believe that going on tilt means completely losing control, this is not the case. It's when players who are usually very tight players begin playing recklessly.

Whenever anyone bases poker decisions on feelings rather than common sense, he qualifies as being on tilt. When you're frustrated, usually from losing a big pot that was yours all the way to the river, you begin to play hands more aggressively. You need to prove to the table that you're still in control and you're getting your money back.

The slow boil is there and the consequences can be devastating. Unfortunately, most players don't get up and take a break—they stay and try to fight their way back to even. But you should always opt for taking that break.

⚡ Alert

When you are about to log onto your favorite poker site, be sure that you are not distracted by television, family members, or anything else that can interfere with your undivided attention—including a bad mood or lack of sleep.

Following are tips to help you handle yourself, and your game, when you start to go on tilt:

- When playing Texas Hold'em, for example, you are usually a three- or four-to-one favorite in any hand you play. That is, unless you flop a royal flush. Therefore, one out of four times you will be up against an opponent who made the wrong call, but who will most likely call their drawing hand all the way to the river and beat you. Now, that's a bad beat, but the adrenaline rush that the player who has just beat you is experiencing is what keeps these bad players coming back.
- Know that when you are running really bad, are severely frustrated, maybe even steaming mad, you aren't likely to calm down anytime soon. This is not the time to continue playing. You need time to clear your head, calm down, and recharge.
- Know that if you're an emotional player, it will be nearly impossible for you to avoid going on tilt at one time or another. Even the poker pros go on tilt. Just look at Phil Hellmuth and Mike Matusow!
- Remember, poker is not only a game of patience and skill, but also a game of luck, which means that you're betting your hard-earned dollars on random chances. And when random chances affect the outcome of your hands, it's time

to tighten up your play and not continue to chase, especially if you're on tilt and praying that Lady Luck's about to turn in your direction.

- Whenever you're steaming, a state that you're not likely to calm down from any time soon, you should remember that tomorrow is another day and give your poker play a much-needed break.

Once you have learned to recognize the signs that you're starting to play on tilt, and learn to accept the negative consequences that bad beats and bad decisions can cause, you will be more mentally prepared to deal with the negative effects. This will only benefit your game and profits in the future.

Mistake: Playing Beyond Your Means

Playing poker online gives whole new meaning to the betting portion of the game. The play is so fast—sixty or more hands per hour—that it becomes mesmerizing. The rake, blinds, and antes can eat you up quickly. Sitting at the computer, it's so easy to keep seeing hand after hand. It's tempting to play loose, to just click that mouse and call, card after card, or suddenly bluff off a lot of chips on a whim. In a casino, a bluff is a major move. Online, you just click the mouse and off go the chips.

Money management can go up in cybersmoke along with discipline. After a while, the chips don't seem real—until you get your credit-card bill. And don't forget the problem of "mis-clicking"—hitting the raise or call button when you meant to hit fold. This happens more often than many players would like to admit. With all these ways to accidentally put too much cash on the line, it's easy to see how players often end up playing beyond their means.

When you play beyond your means, you are playing with a bankroll that you cannot afford to lose. If you do this you are opening yourself up to a whole world of frustration as you try to scrape and claw your way back to even, only to fall further down the rabbit hole.

Anyone can get lucky every once in a while playing poker. And if everyone who played in games above their means didn't win sometimes, you would find yourself playing with people as good and as tight as you are, which could get boring and result in small pots. So you want players who play above their means, as they tend to tilt more often, giving you opportunities to steal the pot.

Fact

The stretch of time a player can run bad can be long, no matter how solid a player she may be, because of the luck factor. True, you are playing to make money, but hopefully you are also playing because you enjoy the game.

Following are tips to help keep your head above water when you're betting in online games:

- A good player does not need as big a bankroll as do beginners, whose skills cannot compete with the more experienced players, and who will therefore make more costly mistakes.
- Play with only money you can afford to lose so that, if you do go broke, it won't have as negative an impact on your lifestyle.
- Play in limit games where you can comfortably afford the appropriate bankroll to support your action. If a $4/$8 game is too rich for your blood, play in a $3/$6, a $2/$4, or a $1/$2 game, or lower.
- If you tend to be a losing player and have no self-control, you'll find yourself in serious financial distress unless you take hold of your finances and play in the play-money games until your game skill and luck improve.
- Aggressive players need larger bankrolls because their win/lose ratios tend to fluctuate greatly.
- Conservative and good players with a firm understanding of the game need smaller bankrolls, since they tend to play fewer trap and drawing hands all the way to the river.

- When playing in higher limit games, if your bankroll appears to be disintegrating, it's time to move down to lower limit games, which takes discipline. Tighten up your play and work on rebuilding your bankroll, regardless of how long it takes.
- Decide how much money you are willing to risk should the cards not go your way. Then stick with your decision and avoid excuses that justify continuing to feed your online account with money you can't afford to lose.

How do you know how much of a bankroll is enough? A good rule of thumb that many online poker players adhere to is a bankroll of about 350 times the large bet. Therefore, if you are playing in a $4/$8 game, you should have $2,800 available. Whatever amount you decide on, only deposit an amount you can comfortably afford to lose. Remember, money management is paramount. Make a financial plan and stick to it. Over the long haul you'll come out a winner.

Mistake: Losing Focus

It is vital that you pay attention during an online or offline poker game, whether you're in the hand or not. An advantage that online players have is being able to observe the play without anyone knowing they are there. When you click yourself into the game, you have a full read on your opponents' play, which is a good move on your part.

Following are tips for keeping you on your toes when you play in online poker games:

- When you observe the game's play, note what opponents play loose or tight pre-flop.
- Note which players are rocks and which will draw to any hand.
- Be aware of aggressive players.
- Create a physical environment without interruptions.
- Only play poker. Do not read, answer e-mail, watch television, and so on.
- Music is fine, but television tends to distract and should be turned off.

- Talking on a telephone, having a conversation with another person in the room, or just about any other activity you can think of is a distraction and should be avoided. Many a good poker player has lost a bankroll that he would have won had his full attention been on the game.
- Use the note section on your computer screen to jot down important information on your opponents' style of play. It helps keep you focused on the game.
- When you observe games that you're considering entering, look for any fish—bad poker players who tend to lose a lot of money, but who also have deep pockets. That's the game you want to play in.

When you are an alert, savvy player who takes every opportunity to observe your opponents' play and distinctive tendencies (such as check-raising, slow-playing, and bluffs), and note which players only play the nuts, you put yourself in an excellent position to come out a winner. Just keep your full attention on the prize: huge pots!

Essential

When you know the screen name of a fish, you can add it to your buddy list. When he logs on and sits in a game, you'll get an alert. Party Poker is one of the online sites that offers this feature to its members.

When you pay attention you'll be in a better position to fold your mediocre hands when a tight player comes out betting. But you won't know this unless you've been observant and have taken good notes.

Improving Your Game

Everyone's game needs improving at one time or another, even a world champion's. You should want to hone your skills on a regular basis to improve your game. If you do this, then you might find yourself the feared opponent at the virtual poker table.

The first step is to figure out where your weaknesses lie. Weaknesses are not just skills you don't have or a lack of experience; distractions and negative influences can also become weaknesses. When you become aware of something that negatively affects your play, avoid it. Take a break, change games, change tables—do whatever it takes to stop it from affecting your bankroll.

Say you're playing in an offline game and you realize that a particular dealer never pushes you a pot. What do you do, stay and hope today will be different? Or take a walk? Take that walk, just as you'd take a break if someone whose mere presence always seems to negatively affect you has entered your online game.

But what if your problem is medium pocket pairs? You see your opponents winning huge pots with them. But whenever you play them, and play them exactly the same way as your opponents play them, you lose, and big. And since these pairs come around every couple of hundred hands, this can be a problem, especially when you seem to get them even more frequently.

If you are in a limit game and must see the flop with a pair under 10-10, fold if you see one over card, especially if you had to take any raises before the flop. If you're in a no-limit game or tournament, don't allow yourself to get trapped unless the only over card is as big a rag as your two cards. If the flop is 7-5-2, and you have 6-6, you may want to see the turn card if you can see it cheaply. But remember, any action you call can end up being costly because, even if you hit your set of Sixes, someone playing the 8-9—or worse, 3-4—has just hit their straight.

Plugging Your Leaks

To find out how big the leaks in your game are, you have to measure how much the leaks cost you. You do this by figuring out how many times you play your hand correctly and lose, versus how often you play it incorrectly and win. But this requires extensive note-taking or an exceptional memory, which many poker players either don't possess or are too lax to care about.

Following are generalized suggestions for plugging leaks that can hurt your game. If you don't take the time to correct chronic weaknesses that have been affecting your game, you will continue to fight to survive.

- Do not fall in love with any two cards by cold-calling all pre-flop raises when you know your hand is probably dominated.
- If you do not get your hand on the flop fold, don't take one more off because the limit is still low. Fold until your game and/or your luck has changed.
- Do not call a bet with your pocket pair when there are over cards on the board.
- Tighten up your pre-flop game to play only the starting premium cards.
- Know how many outs you still have before making any calls.
- Do not raise on the come unless you also have at least a high pair as a backup.
- Do not make calls to "keep your opponent honest" when you are pretty sure you are beat. If your gut instincts tell you that you are beat, you usually are!

Question

How will I know when the leaks in my game need my attention?
You know your game needs some fine-tuning when you continue to lose with the same hands that you play correctly, or when you realize your bankroll is decreasing and you're struggling to get back to even.

When you know, in your heart of hearts, that your hand is the table dog, don't take the time to figure out the "what ifs." Just fold before you find yourself trapped.

Leaks in your game can be costly. So ask yourself what leaks are costing you the most money, then shore them up and continue to be aware of them.

The Virtue of Patience

Some people will say that a lack of patience is the number one problem for most poker players. And without patience, many people can and will end up going on tilt.

If you are the instant gratification type, then developing patience will not come easily. But it's patience that allows you to work around, for example, accepting an unavoidable loss when you did everything right, and not beating yourself up over it. However, no one takes bad beats well, and that holds true for the most patient of players. Possessing patience allows you to react in a more restrained manner versus feeling, and showing, rage and aggression.

E ssential

Being a patient player means that you are able to wait for the outcome of your hand without experiencing anxiety and inner turmoil, unlike the players who scream at their computer, or at the dealer, for that miracle river card.

When playing online, showing aggression is usually done by going all in, or by jumping out of the game abruptly. Always opt for jumping out of the game versus continuing to gamble. Never allow a bad beat to pull you so far off your game that you begin to lose your concentration. To win consistently you need to remain patient and tighten up your game for a while.

Following are a few suggestions for staying patient and focused:

- Be sure you are mentally prepared and psyched before you sit in on any poker game.

- Keep your mind open and your eyes on your opponents so you can learn what you will need to know in order to beat them.
- Be aware of all your outs after the flop before you act. Then know what you will do if your flop doesn't get there.
- Practice in lower limit games to get the feel of winning and losing to help you decide if you can take the pressure of the losses you can experience in higher limit games.
- Only play the hands that stand a good chance of winning after the flop.
- Learn to be able to fold the majority of your hands, if not pre-flop, then on the flop, when the flop cards don't help your hand and there is action.

The goal when playing in any poker game is to increase your bankroll. To be successful, you will have to be able to fold many of your hands on the flop to avoid further losses and patiently tweak your skills. Anyone can become a great poker player if she is willing to put in the time it will take to study, practice, and play the game.

Taking It to the Next Level

So you've gotten really good at poker—both online and in the casino card rooms. You've become an expert at spotting tells, taking notes, and bluffing with the best of 'em. You're winning more than you're losing, and your bankroll has never been more plentiful and secure. The question is, what now?

If you've gotten to this point, you've probably started to wonder if it's possible to make a living playing poker. Believe it or not, it *is* possible, and people are doing it all over the world right now! If you consider yourself lucky and tend to win most of the time, this can be a very lucrative way for you to make a cushy living. However, there is also the downside to consider, which includes playing for hours on end and yet still coming up short. This section covers a few of the important considerations you should review before quitting your day job.

From Offline to Online Professional Poker Play

Today there are just as many online poker players who are learning how to play in offline poker rooms as there are offline players who are learning the ropes of online poker play action. But once you have made the relatively easy transition from offline to online poker, you will find that adjusting to the rules and the mathematical statistics is also quite simple because they are basically the same. The only major difference is this: When playing poker online, you are in your own personal comfort zone; offline play requires a drive to a casino poker room or professional card room in order to buy into a poker game.

⚡ Alert

When you are getting the feel of online poker play versus offline poker play, do it on the cheap before entering higher limit games, as online inexperience can get very costly, especially when you are up against seasoned and savvy on- and offline poker players.

When they first begin playing online poker, offline players have a benefit over online-only poker players: a lot of experience and knowledge in the games that they are playing. This is why more and more offline players are now looking to play online poker for a living.

Is It Right for You?

There are some great perks to playing online poker for a living. You are your own boss. You get to make your own hours. You can wear whatever your heart desires. And you can play from virtually anywhere that has Internet access. However, only about 5 percent of the people who try to make a living playing online poker succeed. (And here you thought this was going to be easy!)

As you can see from televised cable poker tournaments, where the entrants won their seats in an online satellite tournament, not all poker players need qualify for membership into Mensa to consistently win.

Question

How will I know if I'm a good candidate to play online poker for a living?
Ask yourself if you are willing to take the time to recognize the flaws in your game, and then take the time to correct them. If you are not, then don't quit your day job.

There are downsides to playing online poker for a living, and you should be aware of them all before you make any career-altering decisions. If you are not an extremely patient and disciplined player, you may want to reconsider your options before trying to earn a living online. Check out the following points:

- There are no paid vacations, medical benefits, or paid holidays for the self-employed poker player.
- When you're self-employed, FICA and Medicare deductions are at 15.3 percent rather than the 7.65 percent deducted when you're someone's employee.
- Poker winnings are taxed as regular income.
- You need to be able to financially withstand the losing streaks that are inherent in any poker career.
- You need to be mentally prepared to grind it out to pay the bills, which means sometimes having to play all day long in the hope of just breaking even.

If you are not willing to put in at least forty hours of online poker play a week, then think again. However, if you have the discipline, if you are a good money manager, if you never stop learning and looking for tells, and if you have a solid grasp of the games you play, you just might be able to make a profit playing poker online.

The Best Time to Play

When you are looking to make money, you should generally log onto your Internet site of choice to play in games and tournaments during the high-volume hours. Late night games are usually looser, with most hands going to the river. On weekend nights, many players are drunk or have just come home from a night out on the town, so many more players tend to stay in with mediocre hands that they just can't seem to find a reason to fold.

The most profitable time to play in online games and tournaments is from 9 P.M. to 3 A.M. PST on Friday and Saturday night, and from 5 P.M. to 10 P.M. PST Sunday through Thursday night. When you log in during these hours, you are ensuring yourself not only the highest volume of players, but also the widest choice of tournaments, games, and limits.

Grinding Yourself Back to Even

When you are grinding it back to even, you are playing an incredible number of hours just to get back to where you started. This can be quite frustrating and a place that most poker players would rather not find themselves. If you have ever experienced this type of online poker session and found it uncomfortable, nerve-racking, and frustrating enough to put you on tilt, then you may want to reconsider playing online poker for a living.

Ⓔ Fact

Unless you are willing to play as long as it takes to grind it out, and to go online when you can play as long as necessary, you are doing yourself a disservice if you expect to earn a living. As a rule, you should never sit in a game with time restrictions hanging over your head, as it will inevitably affect your decisions and cost you over the long run.

Generally speaking, grinding back to even is a futile, and losing, proposition. After many hours of play, your instincts need to be re-energized, and therefore you will tend to put yourself in more trap situations in the hope that, if you could just win this one pot, you'd be able to log off and get some sleep. However, when your head is clear and you are not tired, you know when it's time to call it a day, know that playing "one more hand" will only trap you into gambling away even more chips.

Whenever you hear that little voice in your head say, "Maybe it's time to call it a day," listen!

All-In Protection

If you plan on earning a living by playing poker online, it is important that you play on a site that offers its members automatic all-in protection. With the all-in protection feature, if you are accidentally disconnected after making the call, a side pot will be started for the players still in the hand, as the hand continues without you. However, should you have the winning hand, the main pot will be added to your account.

E Alert

If you suspect that players are abusing the all-in protection feature, contact your member support services team and report them immediately. You will know this when you see the same players constantly disappearing when they are in the middle of a game that suddenly gets very expensive. This is another situation where taking notes of the screen names of your opponents will come in handy.

Because of cheaters, the all-in protection has been abolished at certain tables and in certain tournaments on some sites to create a completely honest environment where the games cannot be manipulated through the abuse of the feature.

Sit-and-Gos for Profit

The strongest reason to play in Sit-and-Gos is not the money you can win. It is the experience it gives you if you are striving to get into the final three when you play in the larger satellites and tournaments. When you get into those satellites and tournaments, the money you can win can literally be in the millions.

 Question

What should I do if I'm short-stacked in a Sit-and-Go game?
If you have to ask, you should not be playing in Sit-and-Gos for profit. But to answer your question, unless you are dealt A-A, you want to conserve your chips and hope to make it into the final three where the prize money is much better. If not, and the blinds are on you, all you can do is hope you finally catch a break.

When playing Sit-and-Gos for profit, there are four things you want to happen:

1. You want to limp in with many hands.
2. You want to look to hit a great flop as cheaply as possible.
3. You want to gamble as little as possible until you make your hand.
4. You want the short-handed games, because the shorter-handed the game, the more value the good and mediocre hands begin to take on.

Therefore, a K-Jo becomes a very playable hand, especially if the flop comes something like J-5-2 off-suit, where you will have a pair of Jacks with a King kicker.

No one will ever become an overnight sensation playing in Sit-and-Gos. It can take literally hundreds upon hundreds of hours to master your play. But no amount of hours can take away the vital experience this investment of time will bring if you plan on using the higher buy-in Sit-and-Gos as a source of income.

Chapter 14

Knowing When to Fold'em

There are many reasons to fold a hand in a poker game. Maybe your cards are no good, or your eyes are tired from staring at the computer screen. These same ideas apply to your whole poker-playing experience. While poker can be a lot of fun, there may also come a time when you'll decide it's best to turn in your chips—virtual or otherwise—and move on. After all, you *can* get too much of a good thing, and when poker starts to interrupt the financial, social, or other parts of your life, it's time to call it quits.

About Compulsive Gambling

Compulsive gambling is the obvious symptom of an emotional disorder. The emotional factors involved are inability or unwillingness to accept reality, emotional insecurity, basic immaturity, and lack of self-esteem. The gambler finds that he is most comfortable when gambling. Many psychiatrists feel that the gambler has an underlying need for self-destruction.

E Alert

Believe it or not, there is one redeeming aspect of online poker versus the draw poker slot-machine addiction: You can become addicted to online poker while at the same time being a consistent winner. So the online addiction may be more about how your addiction is affecting your family and friends than its effect on your bank account.

Compulsive gambling brings despair and humiliation into the lives of countless numbers of men, women, and children. The compulsive gambler is a person who is dominated by an irresistible urge to gamble. Coupled with this is the obsessive idea that a way will be found not only to control the gambling, but also to make it pay and to enjoy it besides. This disease causes deterioration in almost all areas of the person's life.

E ssential

Compulsive gamblers attempt to be seen as philanthropists and all-around good people. Much of the time such gamblers live in a dream world, which satisfies their emotional needs. The gambler dreams of a life filled with friends, new cars, furs, penthouses, yachts, etc. Pathetically, there never seem to be big enough winnings to make even the smallest dream come true—probably because whatever monies he wins are, to the gambler, sacred.

Are You Becoming a Poker Addict?

According to Gamblers Anonymous, statistics show that 4 to 7 percent of the people who gamble in casinos become addicted to gambling. Statistics also show that you've crossed the line into addiction when you can no longer draw the distinction between gambling money and the money you and your family need to survive.

When you mix the disappointments and excitement that problem gamblers find so irresistible with the convenience and privacy of experiencing them in their own homes, is it any wonder that this combination can be lethal for the gambling addict who has brought her addiction into her home and monopolizes the family computer?

Gamblers Anonymous

Gamblers Anonymous has one primary purpose: to help compulsive gamblers stop gambling and gain back their lives. It's easy to join, with no dues or fees.

The first step to recovery is conceding fully to your innermost self that you are a compulsive gambler. After you've done that, Gamblers Anonymous can help you solve your problems. Help is just a telephone call or e-mail away.

Gamblers Anonymous offers the following questions to anyone who may have a gambling problem. These questions are provided to help the individual decide whether she is a compulsive gambler and wants to stop gambling. Most compulsive gamblers will answer yes to at least seven of these questions.

1. Did you ever lose time from work or school because of gambling?
2. Has gambling ever made your home life unhappy?
3. Did gambling affect your reputation?
4. Have you ever felt remorse after gambling?
5. Did you ever gamble to get money with which to pay debts or otherwise solve financial difficulties?
6. Did gambling cause a decrease in your ambition or efficiency?
7. After losing did you feel you must return as soon as possible and win back your losses?
8. After a win did you have a strong urge to return and win more?
9. Did you often gamble until your last dollar was gone?
10. Did you ever borrow to finance your gambling?
11. Have you ever sold anything to finance gambling?
12. Were you reluctant to use "gambling money" for normal expenditures?
13. Did gambling make you careless of the welfare of yourself or your family?
14. Did you ever gamble longer than you had planned?
15. Have you ever gambled to escape worry or trouble?
16. Have you ever committed, or considered committing, an illegal act to finance gambling?
17. Did gambling cause you to have difficulty in sleeping?

18. Do arguments, disappointments, or frustrations create within you an urge to gamble?
19. Did you ever have an urge to celebrate any good fortune by a few hours of gambling?
20. Have you ever considered self-destruction or suicide as a result of your gambling?

©Gamblers Anonymous International

Though Gamblers Anonymous is based in Los Angeles, California, their Web site offers various resources, including both a national and an international meeting directory. The former is organized by state and the latter by country. No matter where you live, Gamblers Anonymous can offer you some form of help with your problem. Just visit ✍️*www.gamblersanonymous.org*.

The Illinois Institute for Addiction Recovery (IIAR)

IIAR was established in 1979 at Proctor Hospital in Peoria, Illinois. Over the past decade and a half, the Institute has developed a wide variety of services and programs to meet the growing need for hospital-based addiction-recovery treatment in the region.

IIAR developed the first comprehensive, specialized compulsive gambling treatment program in Illinois in 1993. In addition to treatment and counseling for compulsive gamblers and their families, IIAR staff members provide training for professionals interested in becoming certified gambling counselors.

IIAR services are available for men, women, and adolescents. Their comprehensive staff of certified counselors is committed to helping persons with chemical and/or behavioral addictions lead comfortable and productive lives without the use of mood-altering drugs or compulsive behaviors. They achieve this goal by providing a variety of medical and counseling services designed to help both the patient and the patient's family. Available care ranges from modern intensive medical treatment to prevention counseling.

To receive additional information on the programs offered through IIAR, e-mail their Vice President, Addiction & Behavioral

Services, Rick Zehr (eric.zehr@proctor.org), call 1-800-522-3784, or visit ✎*www.addictionrecov.org*.

Do You Have a Compulsive Gambler in the Family?

Perhaps you are not the person in your household with a gambling problem, but instead your parent, sibling, spouse, or child has a problem. Living with or even just having a relationship with a compulsive gambler can put a lot of strain on your life, and you'll likely want to do whatever you can to help the person in trouble. This section offers a number of ways to help your loved one acknowledge his problem and get help.

E ssential

For most of the gambling industry's patrons, gambling is fun and a form of harmless entertainment. For those gamblers who become problem or pathological (compulsive) gamblers, however, it can be a devastating illness that negatively affects every aspect of their lives.

Gam-Anon

What is Gam-Anon? Gam-Anon is a fellowship of men and women who are husbands, wives, relatives, and close friends of compulsive gamblers. You need not wait for the compulsive gambler to seek help before coming to Gam-Anon. Gam-Anon's purposes are threefold: to learn acceptance and understanding of the gambling illness; to use the program and its problem-solving suggestions as aids in rebuilding our lives; and, upon our own recovery, to give assistance to those who suffer.

As the gambling escalates, so does the indebtedness. Desperate gamblers often need increasing amounts of money to finance their addiction. Some parents have mortgaged their homes or sacrificed their life savings to rescue their child. Unfortunately, any financial rescue enables the gambler to continue gambling and eliminates the motivation to change.

More and more parents of gamblers come to Gam-Anon to understand the problem and help their child. Members support and help each other by sharing their experiences, wisdom, and strength. At weekly meetings, parents educate themselves and learn new and appropriate methods for dealing with the gambler. In the process, they learn a better way of life for themselves.

 Fact

In Gam-Anon, the member will experience relief from anxiety by accepting the fact of powerlessness over the problem in the family. The heavy load of responsibility for the gambling problem is lifted and the agonizing guilt in regard to failures is gradually alleviated. The energy wasted in attempts to stop loved ones from gambling can be channeled into more useful methods of problem solving.

Acknowledge the Problem

If there is a gambling problem in your home, the Gam-Anon family group may be able to help you deal with it. According to Gam-Anon, answering "Yes" to at least six of the following questions is an indication that you are living with a compulsive gambler:

1. Do you find yourself constantly bothered by bill collectors?
2. Is the person in question often away from home for long, unexplained periods of time?
3. Does this person ever lose time from work because of gambling?
4. Do you feel that this person cannot be trusted with money?
5. Does the person in question faithfully promise that he or she will stop gambling, beg and plead for another chance, and yet gamble again and again?

6. Does this person ever gamble longer than he or she intended to, until the last dollar is gone?
7. Does this person immediately return to gambling to try to recover losses, or to win more?
8. Does this person ever gamble to get money to solve financial difficulties or have unrealistic expectations that gambling will bring the family material comfort and wealth?
9. Does this person borrow money to gamble with or to pay gambling debts?
10. Has this person's reputation ever suffered because of gambling, to the point of committing illegal acts to finance it?
11. Have you come to the point of hiding money needed for living expenses, knowing that you and the rest of the family may go without food and clothing if you do not?
12. Do you search this person's clothing or go through his or her wallet when the opportunity presents itself, or otherwise check on his or her activities?
13. Does the person in question hide his or her money?
14. Have you noticed a personality change in the gambler as his or her gambling progresses?
15. Does the person in question consistently lie to cover up or deny his or her gambling activities?
16. Does this person use guilt induction as a method of shifting responsibilities for his or her gambling upon you?
17. Do you attempt to anticipate this person's moods, or try to control his or her life?
18. Does this person ever suffer from remorse or depression due to gambling, sometimes to the point of self-destruction?
19. Has the gambling ever brought you to the point of threatening to break up the family unit?
20. Do you feel that your life together is a nightmare?

If you are prone to addictions, especially any form of gambling addictions, then you should avoid online poker at all costs. It is just as addicting as draw poker machines found in casinos—and even more accessible.

Intervention

An intervention is the action taken by family, friends, employer, and/or concerned others to actively assist someone to change unacceptable behavior. The problem areas that an intervention typically addresses are addiction to alcohol and/or other drugs, nicotine, food, the Internet, sex, spending/shopping, and gambling; the need for nursing home or medical care; domestic violence issues; and chronic pain with addiction.

It was once believed that an individual struggling with addiction or resisting changing unhealthy behaviors had to sincerely want to get help. The individual had to "hit bottom" before being motivated to change. This, of course, is not always true.

No person can easily survive without support from someone close to him/her. Interventions are based on this fact.

E Alert

A person will continue to live his life of active addiction or unhealthy behavior when friends and family offer inappropriate support. This type of support typically allows the addiction or behavior to continue. In most cases, family and friends feel that they are protecting the individual, but in fact, they are creating an unhealthy support system for him.

The intervention process addresses the unhealthy support system that allows the addiction to progress. Addiction breeds secrecy and isolation, both for the individual and for those who care about him. The intervention process brings together family, friends, and other concerned persons and creates a support network for each member. The support network in turn engages and empowers the individual to grow and change in a positive way—it does not shame or humiliate him because of addiction or unhealthy behavior.

Did You Grow Up with a Compulsive Gambler?

Compulsive gambling is a symptom of an emotional illness, characterized by low self-esteem, immaturity, instability, and obsessive behavior. Because compulsive gambling is an insidious and baffling illness, some adults have difficulty deciding if they were affected by compulsive gambling during childhood. The following questions (posed on the Gam-Anon Web site, ✑*www.gam-anon.org*) may help you to determine whether compulsive gambling affected your childhood or is affecting your present life.

1. Do you obsess about money?
2. Did family activities revolve around gambling events (sports, cards, lottery, racetracks, etc.)?
3. Have you ever been missing money?
4. Have you ever paid or been asked to pay a parent's debts?
5. Do your parents often argue about money?
6. Were you forced to form an alliance with one parent against another?
7. Did your parents use you as a sounding board for their marriage?
8. Are you afraid to be alone with the gambling parent?
9. Do you feel anxious when the phone rings, the mail comes, or the doorbell rings?
10. Do you feel responsible for the unhappiness in your home?
11. Do you confuse pity with love?
12. Have you ever had problems with your own compulsive behavior?
13. Do you feel more like the parent than the child?
14. Are you unable to remember all or parts of your childhood?
15. Do you care for others easily, but find it difficult to care for yourself?
16. Do you find it difficult to identify and express your feelings?
17. Do you have trouble with intimate relationships?
18. Do you lie when it would be just as easy to tell the truth?
19. Do you feel more alive in the midst of a crisis?
20. Do you think more money would solve your problems?

If you answered yes to some or all of these questions, Gam-Anon may be for you.

☀ Alert

Quitting while you are ahead may sound like good advice, but doing so can cost you in the long run. If you are winning it is probably due to playing well, so why would you want to walk away before exploiting your edge and your lucky streak? You wouldn't and you shouldn't. The key is knowing when to stop when you do begin to lose hands.

The National Council on Problem Gambling

Problem gambling is behavior that causes disruptions in any major area of life: psychological, physical, social, or vocational. The term "problem gambling" includes, but is not limited to, the condition known as "pathological," or "compulsive," gambling, a progressive addiction characterized by increasing preoccupation with gambling, a need to bet more money more frequently, restlessness or irritability when attempting to stop, "chasing" losses, and loss of control manifested by continuation of the gambling behavior in spite of mounting, serious, negative consequences.

Following are ten questions about gambling behavior. If you or someone you know answers "yes" to any of these questions, consider seeking professional assistance by contacting the National Council on Problem Gambling.

1. You have often gambled longer than you had planned.
2. You have often gambled until your last dollar was gone.
3. Thoughts of gambling have caused you to lose sleep.
4. You have used your income or savings to gamble while letting bills go unpaid.
5. You have made repeated, unsuccessful attempts to stop gambling.

6. You have broken the law or considered breaking the law to finance your gambling.
7. You have borrowed money to finance your gambling.
8. You have felt depressed or suicidal because of your gambling losses.
9. You have been remorseful after gambling.
10. You have gambled in order to get money to meet your financial obligations.

For further information, visit ✍*www.ncpgambling.org* or call 800-522-4700.

When Is It Time to Quit?

How many times have you said or heard, "I knew I should have left after I won that last pot"? If you're new to poker and have yet to hear or read this, just give it some time. There are two good reasons, other than an emergency, for quitting your play for the day:

- No matter how good your cards are, you keep being outdrawn on the river.
- You are not playing your best, and you know it. This could be because you're tired, not feeling well, distracted, or going on tilt, or for a multitude of other reasons.

Fact

The Mission of the National Council on Problem Gambling (NCPG) is to increase public awareness of pathological gambling, ensure the widespread availability of treatment for problem gamblers and their families, and encourage research and programs for prevention and education.

Many poker players, whether they play online or offline, feel they can still beat the game, even when they are playing slightly distracted. This may be true in some instances, but be very careful. It's difficult to concentrate when you're not all there.

And it's important that you recognize when you are unable to beat the game. It happens to everyone at one time or another, so think of it as just not being your day, or night, and walk away.

You will also hear the expression "Quitting while you're ahead" said a lot, and it means that if you are substantially ahead, you should quit playing, even if it only took ten minutes to double or triple your buy-in.

If you are a disciplined player who can set a stop-loss limit and, when you hit it, stop playing if you are off your game, maybe that's the right move. However, if the game is good, you have a relatively healthy bankroll, and you feel confident that you can beat the game, keep playing a tight game until you feel the game is no longer any good.

Tips for Balancing Poker with Your Life

One of the main reasons people play poker online is to make money. This is why it is important to remember that we work to live, not live to work. So if you're considering playing poker as a new job, remember that you're not actually spending quality time with the family just because you're now home more often. And if you only plan on playing online as a hobby—a release after a grueling day at the office—be sure not to play online to the exclusion of the people in your life.

Essential

To prevent your online poker play from becoming more habit than pleasure, set limits. Take it a step further by giving yourself consequences should you breach these self-imposed limits. A poker life will quickly lose its allure if you start to lose the people who mean the most to you.

One of the biggest concerns for people who spend a great deal of time playing poker at home is that they tend to consume a lot of junk food and to exercise less than those who wake up every morning and go off to work for ten hours a day. They also tend to have more aches and pains from sitting for hours on end as they become more and more at one with their computers. These are pitfalls to watch for and avoid if you do choose to give online poker a prominent role in your life.

Whether you play poker online or offline for a living or just recreationally, your family and personal life still need your attention. So discuss your poker play with your significant other, and when an agreement has been reached regarding your new occupation or hobby, honor the terms of your agreement.

When you remember that your family always comes first, you won't be left clicking into an online game stressed out from misunderstandings and hurt feelings. The goal is to make your online poker experiences as pleasurable as possible—for you and your loved ones.

Popular Online Poker Room Sites

The following online Internet poker sites are all secure sites that you may have seen advertised nationally if you watch any of the many televised poker tournaments. They all offer real-money and play-money games and tournaments, with many additional perks and features.

Absolute Poker

Absolute Poker is a fully licensed, regulated, and secure site that offers its members features such as express payouts and easy deposits, along with a variety of games. Some of the games include Limit and No-Limit Texas Hold'em, Limit and No-Limit Omaha, and Limit and No-Limit Seven-Card Stud. Absolute Poker also offers an excellent sign-up bonus to all its members, and is definitely worth checking out. The bonus code "BTFBONUS" at sign-up will get you a 100 percent deposit bonus up to $750.

✎ *www.absolutepoker.com*

Bodog Poker

The Bodog Poker experience is complete with one of the hottest communities of members, offering great table and tournament action along with a great customer service team. Game offerings include Limit and No-Limit Texas Hold'em, Omaha High-Low, Omaha High, Seven-Card Stud High, and Seven-Card Stud High-Low.

✎ *www.bodog.com*

CDPoker

This site has an exclusive CDPoker School where you will find eleven different lessons to choose from. Members accumulate CD points based on hours of play during a specific time period. If you get enough points, you can earn a seat in a qualifying freeroll tournament in a World Series of Poker tournament. Game offerings include Limit and No-Limit Texas Hold'em and Limit and No-Limit Omaha. CDPoker also offers a very good recruit-a-friend promotion. You will receive $50 for each qualified referral and your friends will also receive an extra $50 when they open an online account.

✍ *www.cdpoker.com*

Doyles Poker Room

Doyles Room offers its members the opportunity to play against the likes of Doyle Brunson, his son Todd, Mike Caro, and many other poker personalities, when you sign up for the weekly Bounty Tournament. Games offered include Limit and No-Limit Texas Hold'em, Limit and No-Limit Omaha, and Limit and No-Limit Omaha High-Low. The bonus promo code "STW110B" gets you a special mega bonus of more than 35 percent.

✍ *www.doylespokerroom.com*

Empire Poker

Empire Poker is a licensed and regulated, safe and secure online site that advertises prompt payouts and offers its members lots of poker games. The site offers the following games: Limit and No-Limit Texas Hold'em, Limit and No Limit Omaha High, Limit and No Limit Omaha High-Low, Limit/No Limit Seven-Card Stud, and Limit/No Limit Seven-Card Stud High-Low. Empire Poker has been known to be a weak competition site, so if you're new to poker or are experiencing a losing streak, this site might give you a much-needed ego boost. Use the bonus code "EP25BUCKS" when you sign up for a free $25. Use the bonus code "FREEPOKER20" at sign-up to receive 20 percent free on your deposit of up to $100.

✍ *www.empirepoker.com*

Full Tilt Poker

Full Tilt Poker was designed to create the best online poker experience and they are committed to having the safest and most secure online poker site. Games offered include Limit and No-Limit Texas Hold'em, Limit and No Limit Omaha, Limit/No Limit Seven-Card Stud, and Razz. Full Tilt Poker gives its large base of players frequent rewards and some of the best tournament offerings, which usually fill up quickly. Use the bonus code "FTPFREE100" to get a 100 percent deposit bonus up to $600.

✍ *www.fulltiltpoker.com*

Hollywood Poker

Hollywood Poker claims to offer the most technologically advanced poker games with regular tournaments and huge prize pools. The following games are offered: No-Limit Texas Hold'em, Limit Texas Hold'em, Omaha High-Low, Omaha High, Seven-Card Stud, and Seven-Card Stud High-Low. There are approximately 3,500 to 4,500 real-money players using the site during peak hours on any given day. Hollywood Poker provides its members with lightning-fast support for both e-mail and telephone queries.

✍ *www.hollywoodpoker.com*

InterPoker

InterPoker claims that you can play all the great games, with hundreds of others, using their state-of-the-art software. Game offerings include No-Limit Texas Hold'em, Limit Texas Hold'em, Omaha High-Low, Omaha High, Seven-Card Stud, and Seven-Card Stud High-Low. InterPoker may possibly offer the best loyalty bonuses anywhere and you are able to earn them monthly, without having to play any required number of hands or hours of play. And InterPoker does have a prop player program for its players who are willing to start up a new game with their own money, while earning an hourly wage for the time that they played short-handed and helped to hold the game together.

✍ *www.interpoker.com*

Nine Poker Room

Nine Poker players get to enjoy the luxury of a swanky new poker room with all the style and sex appeal of Las Vegas. It's a very secure site and part of a major sports book and casino Web site that has been online since 1997. The following games are offered: No-Limit Texas Hold'em, Limit Texas Hold'em, Omaha High-Low, Omaha High, Seven-Card Stud, and Seven-Card Stud High-Low. Nine.com offers a $500,000 guaranteed freeroll, as well as satellites to win a seat in the World Series of Poker tournament.

✍ *www.ninepoker.com*

Pacific Poker

Pacific Poker's purpose is to provide entertainment to people who enjoy gambling by giving them a safe, fun, fair, regulated, and secure environment. Pacific Poker is known to offer its players excellent Limit Texas Hold'em traffic along with really great overall site traffic and games. Games offered include No-Limit Texas Hold'em, Limit Texas Hold'em, Omaha High-Low, Omaha High, and Seven-Card Stud.

✍ *www.pacificpoker.com*

Party Poker

Party Poker claims to offer more tournaments and bigger prize pools than any other poker site. This is not a good site for the squeamish, the on-tilt player, the inexperienced player, or the player who seems to have only bad luck. Games include No-Limit Texas Hold'em, Limit Texas Hold'em, Omaha High-Low, Omaha High, Seven-Card Stud, and Seven-Card Stud High-Low. Use the bonus code "POKERBUCKS" to gets $25 free on any deposit. Use the code "EXTRAGREEN" to get 20 percent extra, up to $100.

✍ *www.partypoker.com*

PokerRoom.com

PokerRoom.com takes trust very seriously and it is their mission to provide top-of-the-line, secure, online entertainment and support to customers wherever, whenever, and in whatever form they want. Games include No-Limit Texas Hold'em, Limit Texas Hold'em, Omaha High-Low, Omaha High, Seven-Card Stud, and Seven-Card

Stud High-Low. The bonus code "BTF" gets you an extra 30 percent on your first deposit.

✍ *www.pokerroom.com*

Poker Stars

Poker Stars offers the largest poker tournaments and qualifies more players for the World Series of Poker, the World Poker Tour, and the European Poker Tour than anyplace else. In fact, World Series of Poker Tournament Champions Chris Moneymaker, Greg Raymer, and Joe Hechem got their start on Poker Stars. Games include No-Limit Texas Hold'em, Limit Texas Hold'em, Omaha High-Low, Omaha High, Seven-Card Stud, and Seven-Card Stud High-Low. Poker Stars is the largest online poker room in terms of active players, bringing in more than 100,000 players to their site during peak hours.

✍ *www.pokerstars.com*

Titan Poker

Titan Poker guarantees a prompt, personal reply to all questions twenty-four hours a day, seven days a week, from the most professional and efficient customer service personnel in the industry. An interesting fact about Titan Poker is that it is a multilingual poker site, which is more the exception than the rule among online poker sites. Games include No-Limit Texas Hold'em, Limit Texas Hold'em, Omaha High-Low, and Omaha High. Use bonus code "2kroll" for a ticket to their $2,000 private freeroll.

✍ *www.titanpoker.com*

UltimateBet Poker

UltimateBet Poker offers a unique feature called Ultimate Buddy, which enables you to instantly know if any of your poker buddies are online and in what game. The site also features a healthy 40 percent bonus when you deposit up to $200 in your online poker account on their site. Games include Texas Hold'em, Omaha, Seven-Card Stud, Triple Draw, and Crazy Pineapple. UltimateBet has been found to offer the best all-around player bonus rewards to their members, making it a good site to consider when you are looking to join an online poker site.

✍ *www.ultimatebet.com*

Appendix B

Poker Terminology

Aces up

A hand that contains one pair of Aces with an additional pair, or two pair.

action

A player's check, bet, call, fold, or raise.

active player

A player in a hand. Also known as a live hand.

all in

When a player commits all remaining chips or cash in front of them.

all in over the top

Going all in after an opponent has bet.

alligator blood

Someone who plays well under pressure.

all-in protection

Feature that ensures that if you are disconnected while in a hand, you still have rights to the main pot. A side pot is created for continued action from the remaining players.

ante

A forced bet that each player must make before cards are dealt. This guarantees money in each pot before the flop. Most online games do not have antes, just the blinds.

avatar
A computer gaming term that describes the image used to represent a player around the poker table.

baby
A small card such as a 2 or 3.

backdoor flush
When you need the turn and/or river card to make your flush.

backdoor straight
When you need the turn and/or river card to make your straight.

backing into a hand
Drawing two cards that make a hand you were not originally going for.

backup
A card that offers you an additional out.

bad beat
Losing with a hand on the river that should have held up.

bankroll
The total amount of money you are planning to gamble with.

base deal
Cards dealt from the bottom of the deck. It's cheating, pure and simple.

battle of the blinds
When everyone but the big and small blinds folds, creating a heads-up action.

belly buster
An inside straight draw.

berry patch
A game dominated by poor players.

bet for value
Betting to increase the size of the pot, not to make your opponents fold.

bet the pot
Making a bet that is equal to the size of the pot.

bicycle
Also called a wheel; the lowest possible straight, A-2-3-4-5.

big blind
The larger of the two forced bets that are typically found in Hold'em and Omaha games. However, big blinds increase after each round of betting when playing in tournaments. Also see *blind* and *small blind*.

big flop
A flop that makes your hand.

blank
A card on the board, or in your hand, that has no value. Also known as a *rag*.

blind
A forced bet made by the big and small blind hand players who are seated immediately to the left of the button position.

bluff
When a player raises or bets a weak hand to make his opponent(s) think he has a strong hand, and fold.

board
The actual poker table of exposed dealt cards.

boat
Another word for a full house.

bot
Short for robot; an online poker game term meaning with no, or minimal, human intervention.

bottom pair
The lowest pair on the board.

brick and mortar
An offline casino poker room or professional card room.

bring in
To open a round of betting.

brush
A card room person responsible for handling the seating chart.

bubble
The person who is eliminated from a tournament just before the prize money starts being paid. If the final table of a tournament consists of ten players and you were knocked out in eleventh position, you were the bubble, and paid nothing.

bullets
A pair of Aces dealt to your hand.

bully
A player who enjoys playing aggressively, especially when the games have been easygoing.

bump
To raise. Also referred to as *bump it up*.

burn cards
Cards discarded face-down from the top of the deck being dealt. This is done to prevent anyone from being able to determine the next card to be dealt.

bust a player
When you eliminate a player from the game by winning all their chips.

bust out
Losing the hand and all your chips, causing you to be eliminated from a tournament.

button
The round white marker that moves clockwise around the table after every hand to indicate where the new action is to begin.

buy-in
An amount of money you pay to play in a tournament or a poker game.

call
To match the most recent bet.

calling station
A player who rarely raises unless she has the nuts.

cap
The last raise permitted on a betting round in many limit games. Also known as Capitola or Cappuccino.

cards speak
A rule stating that the cards determine the best possible hand and not the player. If a player does not realize the strength of his hand, but turns them face-up for the dealer to read, then the cards rule.

case card
The only card in the deck that could possibly make your hand. For example, if two Queens flop and you are holding one in your hand, and the fourth Queen comes out on the turn or river, that fourth Queen would be the case card.

cashing out
When you turn your chips into cash after leaving a game.

chameleon
A player who varies the style of play from being tight to being aggressive.

change gears
Changing your play from loose or tight as a strategic move.

chase
Calling without a made hand in the hope that your long-shot card will come.

chat
Conversation that you type in the chat box during an online poker game.

check
Reserving the right to see what everyone else does, giving you

an idea of what they may be holding.

check-raise
First you check, then raise, when the action gets back to you.

chop
An agreement between the two blinds to take their chips back rather than playing out the hand heads-up. However, this is strictly an offline option.

client
The term for the software that you download to your computer that allows you to interact with the poker room's servers.

coffee-housing
Distracting chatter at the table.

cold call
To call both a bet and a raise in a single action.

collusion
A form of cheating when two or more players attempt to gain an unfair advantage by secretly sharing information.

come hand
Strictly a drawing hand.

come over the top
When you raise or re-raise a bet.

commit fully
When you put in whatever amount is needed to call the hand without question.

community card(s)
A river card that is dealt face-up and used by all the players in a Seven-Card Stud game; the flop, turn, and river cards in Texas Hold'em and Omaha games.

connector
Sequentially ranked cards that can help make a straight.

counterfeit
A card that does not help your hand because it duplicated a card that was not good for your hand.

cracked
A very common term almost always heard whenever pocket Aces are beat. Here's an example: "My aces just got cracked."

cripple
When one player has the cards that another player needs in order to make his hand, the player must call a bet or a raise with a crippled deck. (Very few of the cards the player needs to make a pair or full house are left in the deck.)

crying call
A call made when a player is almost certain of being beat.

cut
Divide, as in "cut the cards," which the dealer does after they are shuffled.

dangler
An Omaha card that does not fit into the scheme of your other three cards.

dead hand
Usually a misdealt hand. Also a hand dealt to a player who has left the table without first looking at her cards.

dead money
Money in the pot donated by players no longer in the hand. In tournaments, it's the term for a player who has no realistic chance of winning.

dealer
The person who works for the poker room as a card dealer but has no vested interest in the hand. The computer is the dealer when playing online poker.

deck of cards
Fifty-two cards consisting of four suits—spades, hearts, diamonds, and clubs—and numbered from Two to Ten, Jack to Ace. There are thirteen cards in each suit.

Deuce
A Two.

dog
Short for underdog; someone who's a real long shot.

dominated hand
A hand that almost always loses to a powerful hand.

donkey
A bad player, easy money, a real fish.

door card
Common in Stud games; the first card dealt face-up to each player.

double belly-buster
A two-way inside straight.

doubling up
Betting all your chips and winning twice as much as you gambled with.

down cards
Players cards that are dealt face-down and not seen by other players.

down to the felt
Out of money or chips.

drawing dead
When you can't win, no matter what cards come on the turn or river.

drawing hand
Playing a hand that is not yet made—for example, four cards to a flush on the flop or the turn.

early position
The first and second players after the blinds; being in early positions, they are forced to act before the rest of the table.

extra blind
An additional blind that usually comes into play when a new player enters the game and posts or when a player changes seats. Offline it is also when an existing player steps out of the game, misses their blinds, returns before it's their blind, and posts.

family pot
The pot after everyone has called to see the flop.

fast play
The playing of a hand aggressively.

Fifth Street
Also known as the river in Texas Hold'em and the final card dealt. In Seven-Card Stud poker games, it would be the fifth card dealt.

fish
Another term for a poor player who seems to enjoy giving away his money.

flat call
Calling a bet without a raise.

flop
The first three community cards that are dealt face-up in the center of the table in Hold'em and Omaha games.

flush
Five cards all of the same suit.

fold
To relinquish your cards rather than calling the bet.

forced bet
A mandatory bet such as the blinds and antes.

four of a kind
Four cards of the same rank.

Fourth Street
The fourth card after the flop. Also known as the turn card.

free card
A turn or river card that you get to see for free when everyone checks.

freeroll

Tournaments where you pay to get in by playing a designated number of hours over a specified period of time, or where the entry fee has been waived. Also used when a player has a shot at winning an entire pot when currently tied with another player. He is freerolling because he believes he can win the whole pot.

freeze out

A tournament that is played until one player has won all the chips without benefit of re-buys.

full house

Three cards of the same rank (also known as three of a kind), accompanied by any pair.

get full value

When you raise or re-raise with the sole intention of building the pot should your strong hand hold up.

get there

When you have made your hand.

grinder

Someone who plays in the hope of getting even. He is grinding his way back to even in the hope of finally making a profit.

gutshot/gunshot straight draw

Four cards to a straight with the middle card missing. If the card comes on the turn or the river, you've made your gutshot draw.

hand

Your best five cards.

heads-up

When only two players are left in the pot.

high card

The card with the highest rank.

hole cards

The first two down cards in Hold'em and Seven-Card Stud, the four down cards in Omaha games, and the three down cards in Crazy Pineapple poker games.

house

The poker room or casino running the game.

idiot end of the straight

When the straight you have just made is the lowest possible straight on the board. Also known as the ignorant end.

implied odds

The odds that you are getting from the expected calls in future betting rounds when you expect to win if you hit your drawing hand.

inside straight

A hand with four cards to a straight but missing a middle card.

jackpot

An offline special bonus paid to the loser of a fantasy hand that gets beat. In Hold'em it's usually Aces full of Jacks, or better, beaten. In some of the large Las Vegas casinos and Southern California card clubs, jackpots have gotten to be over $400,000. Jackpot money is funded completely by player money, which is removed from each pot, separate from the rake.

jammed pot

To move all-in in a no-limit or pot-limit game. Or, a pot that has been raised the maximum number of raises in a limit poker game.

kicker

The highest unpaired card in your hand, used as the tie-breaker if two players have the same hand. This is often seen with a pair, two pair, and three of a kind. If your kicker is a King and your opponent's kicker is a Jack, you have won the hand.

kicker problems

When one or more opponents have the same hand and the kicker becomes the deciding factor. Also known as kicker trouble.

late position

A player's position, usually referring to the button position.

lay down

Folding a good strong hand that you feel can't win.

legitimate hand

A strong hand.

limp in

To call any pre-flop action. It allows the blinds to see the flop cheaply and usually indicates a weak hand. But if anyone raises, you fold.

limpers

Players who only enter the pot for the minimum bet.

live blind

A forced bet put in by one or more players before any cards have been dealt. The word *live* means that these players still have the option to raise or re-raise when the action gets back around to them. Same as an extra blind.

live cards
Cards still in play if they are not on the board or are in an opponent's hand.

live hand
A hand eligible to win the pot.

live one
A loose player; a fish.

live poker
Poker played in a casino poker room, in a card room, or at home.

lock
A hand that is guaranteed to win a portion, if not all, of the pot.

loose
Describes a player who plays too many hands and does not know when to get out.

made hand
A hand that can't be beat.

main pot
The first pot created during a poker hand. Also known as the center pot.

make a hand
When you get the fifth card you need on the flop, the turn, or the river.

make a move
When someone tries to bluff by betting or raising the pot.

maniac
A loose and aggressive opponent who bluffs often and raises like clockwork.

monster
Similar to a made hand, and it doesn't take much to improve it. Also used when referring to a large winning pot, a monster pot.

muck (n)
The pile of discarded hands and burn cards.

muck (v)
What you do with your losing cards when you toss them toward the dealer.

naked ace
An Ace with no other suited cards.

nit
A very tight player.

no-limit
When a player can bet any or all of their chips at any time.

nut flush
The highest possible flush.

nut flush draw
When you need one more card to make the best possible flush.

nut straight draw
When you need one more card to make the best possible straight.

nuts
Like "In the nuts;" the best possible hand. It can't be beat.

nutted-up
An extremely tight player.

odds
Your probability of making a hand versus the probability of not making it.

off-suit
Originally a Hold'em term describing the two hole cards when they are of different suits.

Omaha
A game where the players are dealt four cards face-down and then share the five community cards in the center of the board; you must use two of the cards in your hand to make a hand and win the pot.

on a short stack
When you have a small amount of chips in front of you.

on the button
The best position at the table, which enables you to act last.

on the come
Betting on a hand in the hope that it will get there on the river.

on tilt
When you are frustrated from a bad beat or several losses and begin to play recklessly.

one-on-one poker
Similar to a heads-up poker tournament, but starts out with just two players who buy in for a specific amount determined by the on- or offline poker room and play until one player holds all the chips.

online poker
Poker played on the Internet via your computer.

open
When the first bet in a new hand of poker is made.

open card
A card that is dealt face-up.

open-ended straight
A two-way hand with four consecutive cards, needing the next card at either end to make the straight.

open pair
Two cards of the same value dealt face-up.

out of position
Having to act before your opponents, putting you at a disadvantage.

outs
Unexposed cards, hopefully still in the deck, that can make your hand.

outdrawn
When someone wins by out-drawing their opponent(s) on the turn and river.

over card
A hole card that is higher than any of the cards on the board.

over pair
A pocket pair that is higher than any of the cards on the flop.

over the top
When you re-raise a very large bet.

paint
Face cards: King, Queen, and Jack.

pair
Two cards of the same value.

pass
The same as fold.

pat hand
A made hand on the flop.

pay off
When you call a bet even though your opponent is representing a hand that can beat you.

peddling the nuts
When you bet a draw hand.

play-back
To re-raise.

play fast
Aggressive betting.

play from behind
Checking with intention of check-raising or re-raising.

play/playing the board
A Texas Hold'em term for when the best five-card hand is the community board.

pocket cards
Cards that only you can see. The same as hole cards.

pocket pair
Two cards of the same rank in the hole, or pocket.

position
The betting order that is determined by where a player sits at the table in relation to the dealer button.

post
When a player is forced to put in a blind bet. This can happen when a player first sits down or when a seat change is made.

pot
All the chips that have been bet during any given hand.

pot-committed
When you are forced to call the rest of your stack because of the size of the pot and the amount of remaining chips you have.

pot-limit
The amount in the pot after each round of betting.

pot odds
The amount of money in the pot versus the amount of money it will cost you to call the bet. Pot odds often come into play when you play drawing hands with one card left to come.

premium hands
The top starting hands for whichever poker games you play.

price
The pot odds you get when drawing or calling.

profile
The information a player may enter about herself, such as hobbies, favorite color, etc.

protecting your hand
When offline players keep a chip, or lucky charm, on their cards to protect them from accidentally being mucked by the dealer or by a player aggressively mucking his cards and accidentally taking your cards along with his. Your accidentally mucked hand will automatically be declared dead even if you have already committed money to the pot.

put/put on
When you mentally put another player on a hand (you imagine another player has a particular hand) to help you decide how to play your own hand.

putting on the heat
Pressuring other players by betting aggressively.

quads
Four of a kind.

rabbit hunting
Offline, when you ask the dealer to show what the river card would have been.

rag
A card that does not help your hand.

ragged flop
Flop cards that are of no help to any of the players.

railbird
A spectator.

railroad bible
A deck of cards.

rainbow
A flop that contains three different suits.

raise
When you increase the amount of the previous bet.

rake
A set amount of money that the house gets for every pot dealt. It is how on- and offline poker rooms make their money.

rank
The value of the card or the hand.

ratholing
Pocketing chips or money off the table after a few wins when playing in offline games. This is a form of cheating and not allowed.

read
The ability to assess another person's hand based on tells.

read the board
Being able to understand the board as it relates to all the possible hands that you can make or that can be made by someone else.

re-buy
The option to buy back into a game or tournament after losing all your chips. This is usually seen during the first thirty to sixty minutes of a tournament.

registration
When you sign up to play on an Internet poker Web site.

represent
When you have the appearance of holding a better hand than you actually have.

re-raise
When you raise the previous raise.

ring game
A full-table poker game with no empty seats. Also referred to as a live game.

river
The final community card dealt on Fifth Street. The seventh card dealt in Stud games.

rock

A tight player who folds often and does not play many hands. So when he does raise, or worse, re-raise, you can bet he has the nuts!

rolled up

In Stud games when your first three cards are all of the same value. Also known as three of a kind.

round of betting

When each player in the hand has acted.

rounder

A professional poker player who usually plays in high-stakes games and tournaments.

royal flush

A hand that contains an A-K-Q-J-10 all in the same suit.

run over

When a player tries to take control of the game by running over top everyone's action with raises, and then winning.

runner/runner-runner

When a player's hand was made when he caught the perfect two cards on the turn and the river.

running bad

When you are on a losing streak.

running good

When you are on a winning streak.

rush

When you are on a winning streak.

sandbag/sandbagging

When you slow play a strong hand as if it is weak in an effort to get as much money in the pot as possible.

satellite

A tournament that does not pay off its winners with cash, but rather with a seat in an up-and-coming larger tournament.

scare card

A card on the board that could mean a monster hand for someone.

scoop the pot

An Omaha High-Low term that describes when you win both the high and the low end of the pot.

scooper

A hand that wins an entire pot.

screen name
The identity you have chosen to use when playing online poker.

see
To call a bet.

semi-bluff
This is a bet or raise that you hope will not be called, but if it is, you have outs.

server
A computer that provides service to an online poker room.

set
Three of a kind. Also called trips.

short stack
The player with the fewest chips at the table.

short-handed
When a full table has thinned down to five or fewer players.

showdown
When the player's cards are revealed after all the action has been called.

side pot
A separate pot created for the remaining players after one player has gone all in.

sit out
When your online seat is held after you have clicked "sit out,"

ending when you return to your computer and click back in.

Sit-and-Gos/SNGs
Similar to a one-table tournament that starts as soon as the required number of players are seated around the table.

Sixth Street
The sixth card dealt in a Stud game.

slow play
When you play a strong hand weakly in the hope of keeping more players in the pot all the way to the river.

slow roll
Purposely taking your time, then showing your winning cards last, just to further frustrate your opponent.

small blind
The smaller of the two forced blinds.

smooth call
To call just a strong hand.

snapped off
Getting called on a stone bluff.

soft play
When one player goes easy on another player at the table, usually a friend or family member,

whom she would rather not run over.

soft seat
An on- or offline game where the level of play is not very good, making it easier for a skilled player to do well.

splashing the pot
An offline expression describing when chips are tossed directly into the pot before the dealer can verify the amount.

split pot
A pot that is shared by two or more players because they have the same hands. This is often seen when playing split-pot poker games.

spread/limit
The betting limit structure, as in a $4/$8 limit game.

steaming
Playing recklessly out of frustration and a bad beat.

straddle/sucker bet
An additional blind bet made by the player to the left of the big blind. This is effectively a blind raise and a pot builder.

straight
Five sequential cards of mixed suits.

straight flush
Five sequential cards all in the same suit.

string bet
An offline term describing an illegal move made when a player goes back to his stack to retrieve additional chips without announcing his intention to raise.

suited
Two or mores cards of the same suit.

suited connectors
Two cards that are sequential in rank and of the same suit.

supernit
A super-tight player.

table stakes
The chips and/or money, if money plays, on the table that can be used to bet with.

take off a card
When you call the flop and will decide what to do after the dealer deals the next card.

tell
A clue or hint that a player unknowingly gives away about the strength of their hand.

Texas Hold'em
A poker game that consists of each player being dealt two down cards followed by a total of five community cards.

Third Street
The first three cards dealt in Stud games.

three of a kind
Three cards of the same rank; a set; trips.

tight player
A very conservative player who only plays the strongest hands.

tilting
Playing wildly and/or recklessly.

time
Offline term used when a player requests some time to consider how she should play her hand. In tournament play, an actual clock is used.

toke
In offline games, a tip given to the dealer after she pushes the pot to the winner.

top pair
The highest pair made on the board. If you have a pair of Jacks with one in your hand and the other on the board and it's the highest card out, you have top pair.

top set
The highest possible set of trips. If you hold a pair of Kings, and a King flops and no Aces hit the board, then you are sure to have the top set.

top two
Two pair, which includes your two hole cards, paired with the two highest cards on the board.

tournament buy-in
What it costs to enter a tournament.

tournament entry fee
A small fee charged by the on- and offline poker rooms that comes out of the buy-in money.

trap hands
When you flop three cards to your straight or flush draw and there's been action and you decide to call, and catch the fourth suited card for your flush draw, or the fourth card needed for your straight draw. Now you are trapped into calling all the action on the turn in order to see if you can catch your fifth miracle card on the river.

Trey
A Three.

trips
Three of a kind; a set.

turbo
A form of poker play where a player takes very little, if any, time to act.

turn
Also known as Fourth Street, the fourth community card on the board.

under pair
A pair in your hand that is lower than the pair on the board.

under the gun
The player first to act in any given round.

underdog
The person or hand not favored to win the pot. Also know as the pot dog.

value
A bet made because you have what you believe to be the best hand and you want your opponents to call.

wait list
A sign-up list for the game, limit, and table you want to play online. Many offline poker rooms also have wait lists that you can call ahead of time to put your name on.

wheel
A straight from Ace through Five.

wired
When your pocket, or hole, cards make a pair.

World's Fair
A very big hand.

wrap-around hand
When the connector cards in your hand wrap around three cards on the board to make your straight.

Chat Room Lingo Abbreviations

A
Ace

bb
big blind

bbl
be back later

brb
be right back

btn
button

cu
see you

cya
see ya

ep
early position

fpp
frequent-player points

ft
final table

gc
good call or good cards

gg
good game

gl
good luck

gl
good one

gn
good night

h/e
hold'em

hl
high-limit

h/l
high-low

ICM or icm
independent chip model

IGHN or ghn
I go home now.

itb
in the blind

ith
in the hole

itm
in the money

J or j
Jack

K or k
King

ll
low-limit

lmao
laughing my ass off

lol
laughing out loud/lots of luck

lp
late position

l8r
later, as in cya l8r

ltr
later

lv
live or leave

mp
middle position

mtt
multi-table tournament

n
nice or no

n1
nice one

nc
nice call

nh
nice hand

nhs
nice hands

nhwps
nice hand, well played, sir.

nl or n/l
no-limit

nld
nice laydown

nlhe
no-limit hold'em

o
off-suit, as in AKo

o8
Omaha/8 or better

omg
Oh my god/gosh!

otb
on the button

pl
pot-limit

plhe
pot-limit Hold'em

plo
pot-limit Omaha

plo8
pot-limit Omaha/8 or better

prng
pseudo-random number generator

Q or q
Queen

r
raise or are

rng
random number generator

rotfl
rolling on the floor laughing

rotfl mao
rolling on the floor laughing my ass off

s
suited, as in KQs

sb
small blind

7/8
Seven-Card Stud/8 or better

sng
sit and go

sos
sit-out sign

STT or stt
single-table tournament

t
thanks

T or t
10

tc
tournament chips, as in 500tc

thx
thanks

TLB or tlb
tournament leader board

tnx
thanks

tp
top paid

tptk
top pair, top kicker

tu
thank you

2

to, too, Two

tx

thanks

ty

thank you

tyvm

thank you very much

u

you

ur

your

utg

under the gun

vn

very nice

vn1

very nice one

vnh

very nice hand

vvn

very very nice

vvnh

very very nice hand

wb

welcome back

wcp

world-class player

wylcwtw

Would you like cheese with that wine?

x

any unspecified card such as a Q-x

y

yes

yghn

you go home now

yhs

your hand sucks

yur

your

yw

you're welcome

Appendix D

Poker Hand Nicknames

A-A
American Airlines/Bullets/
Pocket Rockets/Sticks

As-Ac-8s-8c
Dead Man's Hand

A-K
Big Slick

A-K-Q-J-10
Broadway

A-K-4-7
Assault Rifle

A-Q
Little Slick

A-J
Ajax

A-10
Bookends/Johnny Moss

A-3
Baskin-Robbins

A-2
Hunting Season

K-K
Ace Magnets/Cowboys

K-K-K-K
Four Horsemen/Posse

Kh
Suicide King

Kd
Man with the Axe

K-Q
The Marriage/Divorce

K-J
Kojak

K-9
Canine/The Dog

K-8
Kokomo/Lumber Yard

K-7
Columbia River

K-3
King Crab

Q-Q
Dames/Four Tits/Hilton Sisters/
Ladies/Siegfried and Roy

Qs-Jd
Pinochle

Q-J
Maverick

Q-10
Goolsby/Quint

Q-9
Quinine

Q-7
Computer Hand

Q-3
Gay Waiter/San Francisco
Busboy

J-A
Jack Ass

J-Ko
Bachelor Hand

J-Q
Oedipus

J-J
Fishhooks/Hooks

J-J-5-5
Jackson Five

J-5
Motown/Jackson Five

J-4
Flat Tire

2-2
Ducks

2-4
Lumberman's Hand

2-9
Twiggy

3-3
Crabs

3-3-3-3
Forest

3-8
Raquel Welch

3-9
Jack Benny

4-4
Sailboats/Magnum

4-4-4
Grand Jury

4-5
Jesse James

5-4-3-2-A
Bicycle/Wheel

5-5
Presto/Speed Limit

5-7
Heinz/Pickle Man

5-10
Five and Dime/Woolworth

6-2
Ainsworth

6-3
Blocky

6-6
Kicks/Route 66

6-6-6
Kotch

6-9
Big Lick

7-2
Beer Hand/The Hammer

7-6
Union Oil

7-7
Sunset Strip/Walking Sticks

8-5
Finky Dink

8-8
Little Oldsmobile/Snowmen

9-2
Montana Banana

9-5
Dolly Parton/Working Girl's Hand

9-8
Oldsmobile

10-2
Doyle Brunson

10-3
Weinberg

10-4
Broderick Crawford/Good Buddy/Over and Out

10-10-10
Thirty Miles of Bad Road

Index